# THE 'ROMAN' CATHOLIC CHURCH CULT
# VS
# SPIRIT-LED CATHOLICISM

### By
### Fr. Francis C. Pompei ofm

**COPYRIGHT**
All rights reserved

No part of this publication may be reproduced, stored in a retrieval system or transmitted in any form or by any means, mechanical, electronic, photocopying, recording or otherwise without the prior written permission of the publisher.

**EDITOR**: Trish Pompei

# Dedication

**To all the victims** of abuse and suffering, past and present, at the hands of the clergy and hierarchy, who for centuries have been and are accountable to no one.

**To all Priests**, my classmates and friends, who were ordained and had gifts of the Holy Spirit, but left to get married, and the 'Roman' Catholic Church Hierarchy suspended, ostracized, forbade them from exercising their ministry, while declaring their marriage invalid.

**To all the believers** who have endured the corruption and evil by the 'Roman' Church leadership, yet love Jesus and their Catholic faith and tradition. You are the promised **'Remnant'**.

# INTRODUCTION

As a Franciscan Catholic Priest for 47 years, I have tried with the grace of the Lord and attitude of St. Francis, to declare the **Holy Spirit** as the answer to the evil that has seduced our Catholic faith and its leadership.

For many years, it has caused me much frustration, disillusionment and anger, what Evil has done and continues to do to Catholicism and the clergy over the centuries, with the horrific corruption and suffering it has caused believers and the world.

I personally believe wholeheartedly what Jesus said, that the gates of hell will not prevail against it. Using scripture, especially what Jesus said, taught and did, plus how the early Christians lived, that the Holy Spirit and the gifts of the Spirit manifested 2000 years ago, have and are manifesting today in all believers.

What is contained in this book is not my interpretation or what I believe. Instead, it is the Holy Spirit inviting the 'Roman' Catholic Church hierarchy and institution to a new Pentecost, returning to the early Christians dependence on the **gifts** and **guidance** of the Holy Spirit.

If the Hierarchy and clergy choose not to move in the direction of the Holy Spirit, it will continue to become more and more of a Cult, with the clergy as the Cult leaders.

What will happen to Catholicism and our Catholic faith? The Lord's promise for believers, in the end times, will manifest itself by the outpouring of the Holy Spirit and the gifts of the Spirit to **'The Remnant'** of God, becoming the 'New Catholicism.'

St. Francis emulated this in his life as Jesus transformed him by the Holy Spirit. By doing so, the Church and the whole world could see in Francis what God offers to all of us.

This book will hopefully be a gift and invitation for the 'Roman' Catholic Church to call out and cast out the systemic evil that has infected it. It all starts as it did with St. Francis by his time spent in prayer with Jesus, who transformed him daily into a true Catholic Christian man.

May that be **our** goal whether we are in positions of leadership or sitting in the pews.

One of my favorite passages in scripture is when St. Paul said,

*"It is no longer I who live, but Christ Jesus who lives in me."*

This has been and is one of my goals, even though I fail miserably. May all in our Catholic Church and faith strive to say this about themselves!

# PREFACE

## ST. FRANCIS, REFORMER, NOT A REVOLUTIONARY
(Jul 19, 2019, Fr. Don Miller, OFM)

*In the Testament, St. Francis expresses his deep faith and reverence for priests "who live according to the rite of the holy Roman Church." He goes on to state that even if they were to persecute him, he would still have recourse to them and honor them.*

*Why this respect? (It almost sounds like fawning!). Upon further reading, however, we find that for Francis, every priest—even those who sin—brings him the only visible sign on this earth of his Lord Jesus Christ in the sacrament of the Eucharist. They, and they alone, bring him Jesus.*

*I believe that we can correctly view this matter as Francis' deep faith in and love for not only priests, but also in and for the Church and the* **Sacraments of the Church. It's not a blind obedience or submissiveness to authority on his part; it is faith. And that faith is what makes him a "Catholic" man.**

*Few people would deny that Francis changed both the Church and his society.* **He was not naive. He recognized that both institutions needed a renovation. He loved his homeland—he even went to war to defend it—and his Church, but that did not mean that either was above criticism or reform.** *It was the way he orchestrated his proposed changes that distinguished him as a reformer as opposed to a revolutionary.*

*Francis quietly reformed the Church and the state in his enviably nonviolent way. This is hardly the picture of someone intent on violently undermining the authority of the Church or state.* **He was a reformer, but a reformer in the most nonviolent manner.**

*I believe that upon reading the works of Francis, one finds someone fervently* **obedient to the Church and state, but not opposed to working quietly to improve either.** *There's no railing against or leaving the Church or society. Rather, there must be a deep love for the institutions and a willingness to purify them from within.*

It is with this attitude and love for my Catholic faith and the Church that I have written this book. Lord, make me an instrument of healing, hope, and Peace.

# THE HOLY SPIRIT

Key to real **Reform** and **Change** in the **'Roman'** Catholic Church and Catholicism

# TABLE OF CONTENTS

| | | |
|---|---|---|
| **CHAPTER 1** | THE 'ROMAN' CATHOLIC CHURCH CULT | 9 |
| **CHAPTER 2** | CELIBACY | 24 |
| **CHAPTER 3** | IS THE 'ROMAN' CATHOLIC CHURCH BECOMING A CULT? | 38 |
| **CHAPTER 4** | A HOLY SPIRIT LED CHURCH LIKE THE EARLY CHRISTIANS | 47 |
| **CHAPTER 5** | THE HOLY SPIRIT, OR THE 'ROMAN' CATHOLIC CHURCH IS WASTING ITS TIME | 54 |
| **CHAPTER 6** | THE REMNANT: THE SPIRIT-LED CATHOLICS AND BELIEVERS IN THE LAST DAYS | 68 |
| **CHAPTER 7** | THE CATHOLIC REMNANT'S ATTITUDE TOWARD THE 'ROMAN' CATHOLIC CHURCH | 79 |
| **CHAPTER 8** | 'ROMAN' HIERARCHY AND PRIESTHOOD VS COMMON SENSE | 103 |
| **CHAPTER 9** | WHAT ARE SOME OF THE WAYS THE LORD COMMUNICATES WITH US? | 119 |
| **CHAPTER 10** | THE 'ROMAN' CATHOLIC CHURCH'S NEED FOR A NEW PENTECOST | 143 |
| **CHAPTER 11** | A WARNING AND INVITATION | 148 |
| **CHAPTER 12** | PERSONAL SUMMARY | 154 |
| **CREDITS** | | 158 |

# CHAPTER 1
# THE "ROMAN CULT" CATHOLIC CHURCH

Sex abuse, pedophilia, cover-ups, corruption in the hierarchy, several Popes having illegitimate children, Bishops and Priests guilty of sex abuse of adults, rampant homosexual orgies in Vatican City, schisms, crusades, inquisitions, corrupt banking practices, and the horrific suffering caused throughout history and present day, are the result of Powers, Principalities, and Spirits from the kingdom of darkness that have entered and infected the **'Roman'** Catholic Church.

**POINT**: The underlying issue is that the Evil that has infected the 'Roman' Catholic Church is the same Evil that affects governments and all religions and institutions when unbridled power is appropriated in the hands of one or a few, instead of from, by, and of God. Evil has enslaved human nature to **Power, Money, Sex**, and **Hedonism.**

- *"If you eat of this tree, you will become like God." (Gen. 3:5)*
- *"Understand this Timothy: there will be terrifying times in the last days. People will be self-centered and lovers of money, proud, haughty, abusive, disobedient to their parents, ungrateful, irreligious, callous, implacable, slanderous, licentious, brutal, hating what is good, traitors, reckless, conceited, lovers of pleasure rather*

*than lovers of God, as they make a **Pretense of Religion**, but **deny its power**. Have nothing to do with them Timothy!"*   (II Timothy)

**\*Pretense**: The definition of a **pretense** is a false impression, a false claim, or an attempt to make a falsehood appear true.

- *"Blind guides, Hypocrites all. You are all clean and fair on the outside, but inside you are full of dead men's bones and all corruption."* (Mt. 23:27)

When I professed my vows as a Franciscan with Poverty, Chastity, and Obedience—part of the ritual was to "resist **Power** in all of its forms." The way the world and the 'Roman' Catholic Church are now, I know why. What else I know is that the Holy Spirit and Love is greater than Power.

Jesus gave us the answer and the way through the whole mess, and that is the Holy Spirit. Who then is the Holy Spirit and how do we experience the Spirit's unconditional love, wisdom, guidance, and power?

- *"You will receive power when the Holy Spirit comes upon you and be my witnesses in Jerusalem, all Judea, Samaria, and to the ends of the Earth."*   (Acts 1:8)
- *"The Advocate, the Holy Spirit, whom the Father will send in my name, **will teach you ALL things** and will remind you of everything I have told you."*   (John 14:26)

*You will read these words of Jesus over and over again in this book. It is intentional because they contain the answer and way for the 'Roman' Catholic Church to reform and be made NEW.

**PENTECOST:** They *(men and women)* were **all** filled with the Holy Spirit, praised God in tongues, and then went out unafraid, witnessing and proclaiming Christ crucified.

**THE HOLY SPIRIT**: Trying to describe the Holy Spirit in theological human words is to violate who the Holy Spirit is. It's like trying to scientifically describe the experience of love. It is impossible. God, including God the Holy Spirit, cannot and will never be defined or confined. The only way to know God, Father, Son, and Holy Spirit is not in the mind, but in our spirit and soul by experiencing the divine and becoming one with God.

**JESUS' PRAYER FOR ALL BELIEVERS:**

- *"Father, I pray that all of them may be ONE, as you, Father, are **IN** me and I am **IN** you. May they also be ONE **IN** us, so that the world may believe that you sent me . I have given them the glory that you gave me, so that they may be **ONE**, as we are **ONE**, that they may be **ONE**, so that the world may know that you sent me and have loved them just as you have loved me..." (Jn. 17:22)*

According to Jesus, the Holy Spirit is becoming **ONE** with, and experiencing the Unconditional Love of God. Anyone baptized by the Holy Spirit cannot use words to adequately describe the experience, because the Holy Spirit and the Divine are not known by thoughts or theology, but by experiencing God's love and becoming intimately one with him, as described in John's gospel. This is why those who gathered outside the upper room, listening to the apostles and followers of Jesus speak in various tongues thought they were drunk.

## **EARLY CHRISTIANS:**

This was the whole purpose of Jesus coming— to reveal to the world that the God who created us, loves us, and is now not only with us, but can be experienced in us and in one another.

Becoming one and loving one another is the driving power of the Holy Spirit, as described by Jesus in John's gospel.

- *"I pray Father that they become one. Then the world will know you sent me by the way they love one another." (Jn. 13:35)*

The experience of the Holy Spirit and the risen Christ was now the goal each day. It taught, guided, healed, forgave, and delivered. That is why they gathered together for no other purpose than to experience the Holy Spirit and the Lord with them. From that experience, the Lord created them into his family, loving and ministering to one another.

- *"Unless the Lord builds the city, the laborers labor in vain,"* (Ps. 127:1)
- *"Whenever two or three are gathered in my name, there I will dwell in their midst."* (Mt. 8:20)

**THE POINT HERE** is that they experienced their Creator, Father and their Lord, the risen Christ.

- *"...and the house where they prayed shook, because they were all filled with the Holy Spirit and spoke in tongues,* **and their numbers increased.***"* (Acts 4:31)

To love one another, the Holy Spirit granted them the gifts of the Spirit, **Apostoloi** to lead and **Prophets** to discern the Spirit. They were called by the gifts to teach, preach, preside at the breaking of the bread, heal, and perform miracles. The Holy Spirit gave believers words of knowledge, authority to deliver evil spirits, and praise the Lord in tongues.

The first mentioned gifts provided leadership, guidance, and wisdom for the communities. The latter were to encourage, heal, support, and love one another by those who were given the various gifts.

**HOW WERE PEOPLE APPOINTED TO THESE MINISTRIES?** The believers in each community selected them. When they experienced the manifestation of the **gift** in and through one of their members, it was then that they knew this brother or sister had the Holy Spirit within them to pass through and embrace all who they ministered to. **The community** would join together and confirm what the Holy Spirit had already done.

Then the leader *(Apostoloi)* and the prophets also discerned and experienced that their sister or brother had been given the gift by the Holy Spirit. They appointed and designated them to the ministry. Different gifts were given to different people, but all were given by the same Spirit. This equality was specifically described vividly in St. Paul's epistles with *"many gifts, but one Spirit."*

**The selection was <u>not</u> by a democratic vote, a political hierarchical appointment, nor was it by any one desiring and wanting the gift and position.** No one person appointed individuals to their ministry, but the members of the community they belonged to, experiencing the gifts of the Holy Spirit, leadership, discernment, healing, teaching, preaching, and deliverance in their brothers and sisters.

**EARLY CHURCH FATHERS**: As Christianity flourished in the east and west, more and more communities were established by the **experience** and **guidance** of the Holy Spirit. As the faith spread and evolved, the Church faced more and more heresies questioning who Jesus was, what he was, and even how he was.

Therefore, the Leaders (*Apostoloi*) of local churches began to put into human words who Jesus was and what constitutes the absolutes of our faith, according to their common experience of the Holy Spirit. This is the 'Creed'.

It's what makes us Christians— in our tradition, 'Catholic'. Their teaching was like all teachings of the Church, based on **the believer's experience of the Holy Spirit**. It is the Holy Spirit that is the source of all teaching and guidance**, not men**. Jesus himself condemned this method in the Pharisees saying,

- *"You make man's laws equal to God's commandments and put heavy burdens on people and won't lift of finger to help them… blind guides, hypocrites, all!" (Mt. 23:24)*

**THE ROMAN EMPIRE:** When the Roman emperor Constantine converted to Christianity, it gradually spread throughout the empire. This was a positive influence on the faith, which helped to spread the gospel throughout the world. However, the Christian faith was now **the religion of the empire, meaning that changes gradually occurred**.

People across the empire were sometimes pressured and even forced to conform to the new religion. In so doing, **Christianity became a 'Religion' instead of the movement of the Holy Spirit.** As the Church grew in numbers, it represented the end of small basic communities, becoming less personal in worship, emphasizing more the mystery of God, instead of the experience of the Holy Spirit.

The breaking of the bread slowly became something to be observed and not participated in. The practice of breaking the bread in the course of a meal, like the early Christians, slowly diminished.

**THE 'ROMAN' CATHOLIC CHURCH:** Like all humans, as the Church grew, it was tempted by Original Sin to appropriate power and authority to itself, to be like God and the sole dispensers of the divine.

- **Whether knowing it or not the Roman Empire imposed their political and government structure on Christianity, <u>placing the Holy Spirit under the umbrella of the Church</u>.**

- **Suddenly Christianity became more political to appease both the spiritual and political needs of the people.**

This kind of reasoning opened the door for Evil, as it did in the Garden of Eden, for authority, power, and the gifts of the Holy Spirit to only be in the hands of men who occupied appointed offices.

- Only a bishop could discern the Holy Spirit.

- Only a priest could anoint and preside at Eucharist and hear Confessions.

- Only deacons and priests could preach, perform marriages, and bless.

Now the gifts of the Holy Spirit were no longer given to whomever the Spirit chose, but only to those who held the government appointed offices— the pope, local bishops, pastors, and local clergy.

- The 'Roman' Catholic Church became another institutionalized religion with the dissemination of the Holy Spirit in human hands.

## THE RESULT:

- **Leadership and <u>Clergy In the 'Roman' Church</u> had the office and authority, but many lacked the gifts of the Holy Spirit, instead** replaced by power, dictatorship, fear, threats, designating those who challenge them as suspended, removed, silenced, or a persona non grata.

- Welcome to the **'Roman'** Catholic Cult Church and their Cult leaders!

"Power corrupts & absolute power absolutely corrupts."

Despite this appropriation of the Holy Spirit, **the Spirit has done great and miraculous things over the centuries by those who have been given gifts of the Holy Spirit and live by their personal relationship with Jesus.**

At the same time, the corruption of the system by people who held the offices, but not having the gifts of the Holy Spirit, resulted in corruption of the papacy, the episcopacy, the clergy, and the believers, with illegitimate children, crusades, schisms, wars, inquisitions, murder, rape, burning/hanging heretics, sex abuse, genocide, and the list goes on.

Granted we are all sinners, but I wonder if Christians and all Christian denominations would have sinned less and loved more if their daily guide was their experience of Jesus and the Holy Spirit in themselves and with their brothers and sisters.

- **I wonder** if whenever we gathered together with our brothers and sisters, we would have been filled more with God's embrace than theology and business.

- **I wonder** if we experienced the Holy Spirit through acknowledging one another's gifts, would we have been bonded together in mutual love, like the early Christians.

- **I wonder** if we would have healed and forgiven each other more, settling our differences, because we would have learned how by the Holy Spirit.

- **What do you think?**

## POPE FRANCIS POINTS OUT THE SYSTEMIC EVIL INFECTING THE 'ROMAN' CATHOLIC LEADERSHIP: POWER
*(NCR, December 21, 2020, Joshua J. McElwee)*

**ROME** — *Pope Francis Dec. 21, 2020, urged the bishops and cardinals who lead the Vatican's bureaucracy not to be in conflict with one another, warning that the Catholic Church can become **polarized** if the prelates appear always at odds.*

*In an annual pre-Christmas meeting that Francis has frequently used to upbraid his top Vatican officials, the pontiff acknowledged that the church may be in crisis due to scandals "past and present" but said crisis should not be confused with conflict.*

"Crisis generally has a positive outcome, whereas conflict always creates discord and competition, an apparently irreconcilable antagonism that separates others into friends to love and enemies to fight," the pope told the prelates.

"When the church is viewed in terms of conflict — right versus left, progressive versus traditionalist — she becomes fragmented and polarized, distorting and betraying her true nature," said Francis.

"[The church] must **never** become a body in conflict, with winners and losers, for in this way she would spread apprehension, become more rigid and less synodal," the pope said.

**In 2014, he told the bishops and cardinals about 15 "spiritual sicknesses" he said he had witnessed among them. In 2016, Francis lashed out at high-level prelates he said had been opposing his efforts to reform the Vatican, calling them a "malevolent resistance."**

This year, (2020), Francis took a gentler tack. He reflected first on the difficulties faced by many during the ongoing coronavirus pandemic, saying it offered the church an opportunity to reflect on "the meaning of a crisis."

The pope then gave examples of biblical figures who had come out of crises stronger, citing Abraham, Moses, Elijah, St. Paul and Jesus. He said their example "warns us against judging the church hastily on the basis of the crises caused by scandals past and present."

Francis told the Vatican officials that they should not seek to hide from crises, but allow them to bring out needed changes.

"Everything evil, wrong, weak and unhealthy that comes to light serves as a forceful reminder of our need to die to a way of living, thinking and acting that does not reflect the Gospel," said the pontiff.

Referencing his own seven-year effort to reorganize the Vatican bureaucracy in conjunction with his advisory Council of Cardinals, **the pope also said that efforts to renew the church cannot be like "putting a patch on an old garment**, or simply drafting a new Apostolic Constitution."

"The church is always an earthen vessel, precious for what it contains and not for the way it may appear," said Francis. **"These days it seems evident that the clay of which we are made is chipped, damaged and cracked."**

"We have to strive all the more, lest our frailty become an obstacle to the preaching of the Gospel rather than a testimony to the immense love with which God, who is rich in mercy, has loved us and continues to love us," said the pope.

If we read between the lines, Pope Francis' is admonishing the prelates about the polarization and discord they are causing in the church and the faithful. He then points out that those Cardinals and Bishops who have succumbed to this self-righteous power, are responsible for what he calls, "malevolent resistance" opposing his efforts to **reform** the Vatican.

The Holy Father's confronting the evil that has cursed the 'Roman' Catholic Church and its leadership for centuries, is at the heart of this book. Jesus, scripture, and the early Christian communities led by the Holy Spirit, will

- Call it out,
- Cast it out,
- And the Holy Spirit 'Make all things New'

I am not a heretic, rebel, revolutionary, or radical liberal. I am a Catholic, baptized with the Holy Spirit, and believe the Creed as the absolute truth with all my heart. I also believe in the leadership, gifts of the Holy Spirit, and ministries of the Catholic Church. I believe together with all gifted believers, shepherds, priests, prophets, teachers, preachers, healers, and those with the gift of discernment and words of knowledge.

As I watch the leadership and institutional structures of the **'Roman'** Catholic Church dry up like an old wine skin, from the sexual abuse of minors, nuns, and others, and the cover-ups by Bishops and Priests, I must confess that after over four decades of priesthood, I sometimes am ashamed of being a **'Roman'** Catholic priest.

The Roman Empire superimposed its government and political structure on early Christianity's trust and reliance on the Holy Spirit as their advocate and guide, to lead and minister to one another. Yet, I trust and know that the Holy Spirit will rise from the ashes, and the new wine will spring forth in a new wine skin.

I believe that the new wine will flow when we, like our evangelical brothers and sisters who are flourishing (*with many former Catholics joining, experiencing the Holy Spirit, given and using their gifts of the Spirit*) are all baptized with the Holy

Spirit, like the disciples were at Pentecost and Paul on the road to Damascus.

In the world, as it is today, I believe all Christians of any denomination who put the experience and gifts of the Holy Spirit at the center of their worship and community will bear much 'fruit.' **I believe, like the early Christians, that only those who have the gifts of the Spirit, recognized and experienced by the community, be appointed to the Office.**

In short, **Pope John the XXIII** was the real Prophet for these end times through proclaiming that the Church needed a **New Pentecost.** The Ecumenical Council involved other religions and people from all walks of society to discern God's will. It was not only for the Catholic Church, but the whole world. I also believe, **because the Hierarchy has not listened and discerned the direction of the Holy Spirit these past sixty years, our leadership and the institutional church, established by the Roman Empire is in the shambles that they have created and perpetuate**.

There is no need to be offended, defensive, or guilty by all this, but instead face reality, seek a new Pentecost and choose to trust in the Lord and let go of the old wine skin. Release the power, control, and structures that guided us for centuries that aren't bearing fruit any more.

Jesus said, "If the fig tree does not bear fruit, cut it down." **In other words, stop doing it that way!** Instead, look forward, seek and ask for the gifts of the Holy Spirit and keep our spiritual ears and eyes open for the movements of the Holy Spirit that will bear fruit.

**Remember**, there are two Baptisms—the Baptism with water, and the Baptism of the Holy Spirit. If you have not experienced the Baptism of the Holy Spirit, like the early Christians did at Pentecost when the room shook, then keep praying and asking for it. When you and all in your community and parish do, you are on the greatest journey and adventure of your lives. It ends with eternal life... *I Say Alleluia & Come Holy Spirit!*

# CHAPTER 2

# CELIBACY

## POLITICAL POWER AND CONTROL OF THE SYSTEM

### A BRIEF HISTORY OF CELIBACY IN THE CATHOLIC CHURCH

### First Century
Peter, the first pope, and the apostles that Jesus chose were, for the most part, married men. The New Testament implies that women presided at Eucharistic meals in the early church.

### Second and Third Century
Age of Gnosticism: light and spirit are good, darkness and material things are evil. A person cannot be married and be perfect. However, most priests were married.

### Fourth Century
**306**-Council of Elvira, Spain, decree #43: a priest who sleeps with his wife the night before Mass will lose his job.
**325**-Council of Nicea: decreed that after ordination a priest could not marry.
**352**-Council of Laodicea: women are not to be ordained. This suggests that before this time there was ordination of women.
**385**-Pope Siricius left his wife in order to become pope, decreed that priests may no longer sleep with their wives.

### Fifth Century
**401**-St. Augustine wrote, "Nothing is so powerful in drawing the spirit of a man downwards as the caresses of a woman."

## Sixth Century
**567**-2nd Council of Tours: any cleric found in bed with his wife would be excommunicated for a year and reduced to the lay state.
**580**-Pope Pelagius II: his policy was not to bother married priests as long as they did not hand over church property to wives or children.
**590-604**-Pope Gregory the Great said that all sexual desire is sinful in itself (meaning that sexual desire is intrinsically evil?).

## Seventh Century
France: documents show that the majority of priests were married.

## Eighth Century
St. Boniface reported to the pope that in Germany almost no bishop or priest was celibate.

## Ninth Century
**836**-Council of Aix-la-Chapelle openly admitted that abortions and infanticide took place in convents and monasteries to cover up activities of celibate clerics.
**St. Ulrich, a holy bishop, argued from scripture and common sense that the only way to purify the church from the worst excesses of celibacy was to permit priests to marry.**

## Eleventh Century
**1045**-Benedict IX dispensed himself from celibacy and resigned in order to marry.
**1074**-Pope Gregory VII said anyone to be ordained must first pledge celibacy: priests [must] first escape from the clutches of their wives.

**1095**-Pope Urban II had priests wives sold into slavery, children were abandoned.

## Twelfth Century
**1123**-Pope Calistus II: First Lateran Council decreed that clerical marriages were invalid.

## Fourteenth Century
**Bishop Pelagio complains that women are still being ordained and hearing confessions**.

## Fifteenth Century
Transition; 50% of priests are married and accepted by the people.

## Sixteenth Century
**1545-63**-Council of Trent states that celibacy and virginity are superior to marriage.

## Twentieth Century
**1930**-Pope Pius XI: sex can be good and holy.

**1951**-Pope Pius XII: married Lutheran pastor ordained catholic priest in Germany.

**1962**-Pope John XXIII: Vatican Council II; vernacular; marriage is equal to virginity.

**1966**-Pope Paul VI: celibacy dispensations.

**1970s- Ludmilla Javorova and other Czech women ordained to serve needs of women imprisoned by Communists.**

**1978**-Pope John Paul II: puts a freeze on dispensations.

**1983**- New Canon Law. 1980-Married Anglican/Episcopal pastors are ordained as catholic priests in the U.S.; also in Canada and England in 1994.

## Popes who were married
- St. Peter, Apostle
- St. Felix III 483-492 (2 children)
- St. Hormidas 514-523 (1 son)
- St. Silverus (Antonia) 536-537
- Hadrian II 867-872 (1 daughter)
- Clement IV 1265-1268 (2 daughters)
- Felix V 1439-1449 (1 son)

## Popes who were the sons of other popes, other clergy

| Name of Pope | Papacy | Son of |
| --- | --- | --- |
| St. Damascus I | 366-348 | St. Lorenzo, priest |
| St. Innocent I | 401-417 | Anastasius I |
| Boniface | 418-422 | son of a priest |
| St. Felix | 483-492 | son of a priest |
| Anastasius II | 496-498 | son of a priest |
| St. Agapitus I | 535-536 | Gordiaous, priest |
| St. Silverus | 536-537 | St. Homidas, pope |
| Deusdedit | 882-884 | son of a priest |
| Boniface VI | 896-896 | Hadrian, bishop |

| | | |
|---|---|---|
| John XI | 931-935 | Pope Sergius III |
| John XV | 989-996 | Leo, priest |

## Popes who had illegitimate children after 1139

| | | |
|---|---|---|
| Innocent VIII | 1484-1492 | several children |
| Alexander VI | 1492-1503 | several children |
| Julius | 1503-1513 | 3 daughters |
| Paul III | 1534-1549 | 3 sons, 1 daughter |
| Pius IV | 1559-1565 | 3 sons |
| Gregory XIII | 1572-1585 | 1 son |

## History sources:

*Oxford Dictionary of Popes; H.C. Lea History of Sacerdotal Celibacy in the Christian Church 1957; E. Schillebeeckx The Church with a Human Face 1985; J. McSorley Outline History of the Church by Centuries 1957; F.A.Foy (Ed.) 1990 Catholic Almanac 1989; D.L. Carmody The Double Cross - Ordination, Abortion and Catholic Feminism 1986; P.K. Jewtt The Ordination of Women 1980; A.F. Ide God's Girls - Ordination of Women in the Early Christian & Gnostic Churches 1986; E. Schüssler Fiorenza In Memory of Her 1984; P. DeRosa Vicars of Christ 1988.*

# CELIBACY: MYTHS AND FACTS

**Myth**: All priests take a vow of celibacy.
**Fact**: Most priests do not take a vow. It is a promise made before the bishop.

**Myth**: Celibacy is not the reason for the vocation shortage.
**Fact**: A 1983 survey of Protestant churches shows a surplus of clergy; the Catholic Church alone has a shortage.

**Myth**: Clerical celibacy has been the norm since the Second Lateran Council in 1139.
**Fact**: Priests and even popes still continued to marry and have children for several hundred years after that date. In fact, the Eastern Catholic Church still has married priests.

**In the Latin Church, one may be a married priest if:**
One is a Protestant pastor first; or if one is a life-long Catholic but promises never again to have sexual relations with one's wife.

**Myth**: The vocation shortage is due to materialism and lack of faith.
**Fact**: Research (1985 Lilly endowment): there is no evidence to support loss of faith as a reason for lesser vocations.

**CELIBACY:** is unnatural and psychologically damaging. It is a direct assault on the word of God that he created humans, female and male, for the need of intimacy, companionship, and procreation.

It was and continues to be the political way for the male dominated hierarchy to cement their control over the financial and corrupt practices that threatened their position of power to be the sole disseminators of the Holy Spirit and sacraments, as well as a way to cover their clandestine sexual immorality.

A reminder, that this was the 'Roman' influence on institutionalizing the church and believers into a religious political structure.

**Celibacy was and is a 'promise'** forced on men, by men in power. Since its inception it gradually became mandatory without exception for any man desiring to be a Priest in the 'Roman' Catholic Church. This was and has never been demanded or required by Jesus. Most of his apostles, disciples, and holy women were married.

This was and is a blatant attack on human freedom and the primacy of 'Conscience'.

### RESULTS:

- The immorality of the clergy, sex abuse of minors, pedophilia, women, illegitimate children by Popes, abortions, murder, torture, fornication, and the list goes on

- Priests had and have to deal with the impossible daily struggle with sexual chastity. Seminaries never taught how specifically to do it, except pray and make a daily holy hour. That is good, there's no doubt about it, but what are you going to do the other twenty three hours when others who you are attracted to and they you, are in your view every day all day. Celibacy is unnatural!

*Does anybody know the struggle forced celibacy does to a person? You have to listen all day to people's complaints and preside at all the liturgies and sacraments, visit the sick, weddings, baptisms, and never ending funerals, preach, fix roofs, pay bills, meetings, hire and oversee staff. Then, at the end of the day you retire to an empty house and an empty bed with no one to love or be loved by.

- Jesus performed his ministry for 3 years. Priests are expected to live celibate priesthood their whole life, 5, 10, 25, 50 years, that's 18,250 days. That is the definition of **LONELINESS** that human words cannot express and married people can never imagine or understand.

- Think of the number of believers over the centuries who were given specific gifts of the Holy Spirit but unable to exercise them because of the **'Roman'** Church's male dominated hierarchy, requiring only celibate men to be ordained. I guess it is unfortunately true that Power corrupts.

- Why is it that so many men that are ordained leave the Priesthood?

- Why is it when they do, if they marry, they are persona non grata and can no longer exercise their gifts of the Holy Spirit in the 'Roman' church, and if they do, it is considered illicit? Can you imagine the number of good and holy Priests we have lost over the centuries?

- Can you imagine the anger of priests whose classmates and priest friends have left and been unable to function, suspended, ignored, and their marriage considered scandalous?

- The incredible anguish and anger is off the charts when good men with pronounced gifts have no desire to be celibate, but in order to answer the Lord's call to be a Priest, have to sublimate and fight with their natural desires for intimacy, to love and be loved by another.

   Many in the hierarchy who may be called to celibacy have no idea of the struggle to live an unnatural life that you had no choice in living.

- Celibacy is a gift of the Spirit, as is the call to marriage and the single life. Gifts cannot be mandated, so it is from a deep respect for the gift of celibacy that it be made optional, as with the early Christians, and not forced upon those who do not feel called in this way.

Jesus condemned this mentality in the Pharisees.

- *"You put heavy burdens on people, but don't lift a finger to help them." (Mt. 23:4)*

- *"You make man's laws equal to God's commandments" (Mt. 23:6)*

# **GOOD AND FAITHFUL PRIESTS: THE UNTOLD STORY**

The sexual abuse of children and adults by the clergy is horrific, as stated before, and left indelible scars that have destroyed their victim's lives.  I lived with three priests who were later defrocked, and I had seven classmates from the seminary who were also defrocked, three of them in jail, one for twenty three years, and one guilty for over fifty counts of abuse of boys only a couple years after he was ordained.

We've heard from the faithful and hierarchy what the sex abuses of the clergy have done to the Catholic church, it's credibility and moral authority, but has anybody given a minutes thought as to what it has done to priests who have been faithful, chaste, celibate, and served both young and old; healing, counseling, teaching, and ministering the Lord and the Gospel?

My intention here is to finally give a voice to all of us priests who have remained faithful to the commitment we made to Jesus and the Gospel on ordination day, and for many years, sexually abusing **nobody.**

**Do the hierarchy and the faithful have any idea what these sexual predators have done to us who are still in the trenches, committed to the Lord and those entrusted to us?**

I can forgive these predators and have, and I will not judge them as to whether they go to heaven or hell. That's up to the God who created them. However, I have an abundance of anger, as I believe most good and faithful priests do, that wants to hold them accountable for what they have done to us personally, to our commitment, our priesthood, ministry, and even our livelihood.

- All any one has to do is make an allegation and even though it may be false, it makes people suspicious, destroys our reputation, and makes us vulnerable to anyone who wants to retaliate or seek revenge on all priests; guilt by association.

- Most of the ministry with youth takes place in small groups or one on one. Predator priests have stolen that from us. I taught high school for ten years and loved it and my students. But I would put my priesthood, ministry and livelihood at risk if I taught again. If I gave a student a bad grade or disciplined them, all they would have to do is make an allegation that I touched them or simply put my arm around them. Whether I did or not doesn't matter. Their allegation would have removed me from teaching, suspended my ministry, and tarnished or ruined my reputation, not to mention my future livelihood with no income.

- Some Bishops distance themselves from any priest who has an allegation against them and offer no support or financial assistance if it goes to trial. Why, out of fear that they may be accused of a cover-up.

- **Congratulations** to the beautiful and inspiring theology of 'Celibacy' fed to us for centuries by the hierarchy. You created these sexual predators. **They are your sons!**

To my brother priests who have endured and continue to be falsely accused and vulnerable to attacks, with ministry always suspect, hang in there and stay the course, trusting in the Holy Spirit and the promise that our reward will be great in heaven.

*"Blessed are you, when they persecute you and speak all kinds of evil against you for my sake. Your reward in heaven will be great." (Mt. 5:11)*

## IS IT REALLY ABOUT A SHORTAGE OF PRIESTS?

There is a 'shortage' of priests for the 'Roman' church because of placing all the gifts of the Holy Spirit under the authority of one man, the Priest, Bishop, i.e. hierarchy.

- **If your lens and focus is on the sacraments that only Priests can perform**, then there is an emphasis on the **shortage of clergy** and the need for more vocations to secure their authority.

- **If your lens is focused on people and not priesthood**, there is a <u>shortage of ministry</u>: Healing, Teaching, Preaching, Deliverance, Discernment, Words of knowledge, Prophecy, and being baptized with and experiencing the Holy Spirit.

This is why 'Roman' Catholics are leaving and joining evangelical churches that are centered on experiencing and being led by the Holy Spirit. Members who are recognized with the various gifts of the Holy Spirit *(Those listed above)* are leading their community and also ministering to each other with them.

# DOES EVERY PRIEST HAVE ALL THESE GIFTS? NOT ACCORDING TO THE WORD OF GOD!

*"**12** Now about the gifts of the Spirit, brothers and sisters, I do not want you to be uninformed. ² You know that when you were pagans, somehow or other you were influenced and led astray to mute idols. ³ Therefore I want you to know that no one who is speaking by the Spirit of God says, "Jesus be cursed," and no one can say, "Jesus is Lord," except by the Holy Spirit.*

*⁴ There are different kinds of gifts, but the same Spirit distributes them. ⁵ There are different kinds of service, but the same Lord. ⁶ There are different kinds of working, but in all of them and in everyone it is the same God at work.*

*⁷ **Now to each one the manifestation of the Spirit is given for the common good.** ⁸ **To one** there is given through the Spirit a message of wisdom, **to another** a message of knowledge by means of the same Spirit, ⁹ **to another** faith by the same Spirit, **to another** gifts of healing by that one Spirit, ¹⁰ **to another** miraculous powers, **to another** prophecy, **to another** distinguishing between spirits, **to another** speaking in different kinds of tongues, and **to still another** the interpretation of tongues.*

*¹¹ **All these are the work of one and the same Spirit, and he distributes them to each one, just as he (The Holy Spirit) determines."** (1 Cor. 12:1)*

I have intentionally used **Bold** fonts to emphasize that the gifts of the Holy Spirit are given to many in the community and not just the Priest. They are also given for the common good of their brothers and sisters. According to the word of God, the gifts are given by the Spirit, not men. This experience of the early Christians is part of our Catholic Tradition and confirmed in scripture.

# CHAPTER 3

# IS THE 'ROMAN' CATHOLIC CHURCH BECOMING A CULT?

## WHAT MAKES UP A CULT?

- A charismatic leader, who increasingly becomes an object of worship and replaces the members' beliefs with his own, resulting in the groups loss of individual freedom.

- The cult leader, who has no meaningful accountability, becomes the single most defining element of the group and its source of power and authority.

There is a process of indoctrination or education in use that can be seen as coercive persuasion or thought reform, commonly called 'brainwashing'.

## HERE ARE WARNING SIGNS OF A LEADER WITH THE OFFICE, BUT NOT THE GIFTS.

- Absolute authoritarianism without meaningful accountability

- No tolerance for questions or critical inquiry

- There is no legitimate reason for members to leave. Former followers are always wrong in leaving because the Leader and the community have the divine truth.

Those who leave are not considered a member of the True faith, excommunicated or considered fallen away.

- Followers feel they can never be 'good enough', driven by guilt if they disagree with the leader and fear of reprisals from the community and even God.

- The leader and group are always right.

- The group/leader is the exclusive means of knowing 'Truth' or receiving Divine revelation. No other process of discovery is really acceptable or credible. They are the absolute power, accountable to no one, because they have been divinely appointed by others who believe they also have been divinely appointed.

Have the Bishops and Pastors become the Cult leaders, imposing their own interpretation of the gospel, liturgical protocols and rubrics on believers, making their laws *(Manmade)* equal to God's commandments and convincing them they are divinely inspired?

**EXAMPLE #1**

## IN CAME LATIN, INCENSE AND BURNED BOOKS, OUT WENT HALF THE PARISHIONERS POST-VATICAN II NORTH CAROLINA CATHOLICS SEEK A SPIRITUAL HOME

*National Catholic Reporter, Jan 27, 2021*
*by Peter Feuerherd*

Religion scholar Maria Lichtmann felt a strangeness overcome St. Elizabeth of the Hill Country Parish in Boone, North Carolina, four years ago.

**Fr. Matthew Codd**, the then-pastor at St. Elizabeth's, was joined by a group of seminarians who went through the church's theology library and removed books deemed heretical, including those of spiritual writers Henri Nouwen and Thomas Merton. The books were later burned, she was told by a parish staff member.

Lichtmann, a retired religious studies professor at Appalachian State University, left the region in part, she told NCR, because of the changes in the parish. She now lives in Georgia.

"I felt it was a lost cause," she said about St. Elizabeth's.

The spirit of hyper-orthodoxy in parish leadership continued, noted Lichtmann, after **Codd was replaced in July 2019 by <u>Fr. Brendan Buckler.</u>**

Nearing 18 months since Buckler arrived, a few dozen now gather every other Sunday at a car restoration shop shared by a hospitable non-Catholic, the husband of a parishioner.

The informal Mass in the auto shop is necessary, parishioner Karen James told NCR, because "people have no alternative," as the nearest Catholic parish is at least 45 minutes to an hour's drive away. Many parishioners — she estimates about half of 300 active churchgoers who were there when Buckler began — have fled to local Protestant congregations or remain at home, sometimes catching a livestreamed Mass from Charlotte.

The Charlotte Diocese is not alone. While Pope Francis preaches an accompaniment for all spiritual seekers and castigates clericalism — he once described young priests who put a premium on enforcing church regulations as **"little monsters"** — seminaries in the U.S. continue to graduate priests for ordination who look not to Francis, but to Pope John Paul II for inspiration. It is a quiet, awkward and uneasy kind of **schism i**n church practice and discipline.

**They are told that Pope Francis is failing to proclaim church teaching, that most bishops are lacking in orthodoxy, and that it will be up to new, younger priests to rescue the church from its shortcomings.**

"They want certainty. They want answers," she said, noting that they prefer to gloss over complicated issues of moral theology and other concerns. **They also prefer the power granted to pre-Vatican II clergy and look forward to running parishes on their own terms.**

Lichtmann also noted that Buckler made sure there were no more girl altar servers, and at times he was accompanied by six male servers, setting a sign that pre-Vatican II ritual was to be the norm among the Catholics of Boone. **Lay ministers to the sick and homebound were eliminated, replaced by Buckler.**

St. Elizabeth's parish now features three Masses in English each week, one in Spanish, and **four in Latin and celebrated in the pre-Vatican II style, with the priest facing the altar instead of the congregation.** "He is taking us back to pre-Vatican II," Mary Benson Farthing, a former parishioner, said. She now goes to Mass at another Catholic parish 25 miles away.

Letters of complaint have been Recipients included Bishop Jugis, Archbishop Gregory Hartmayer of Atlanta, the metropolitan for the region, and Archbishop Christophe Pierre, the apostolic nuncio. **No one responded to her letters.** Buckler, Codd and Jugis declined to speak to NCR for this article.

**EXAMPLE #2**

## HAVE THE LAITY BEEN TRAINED BY THE CLERGY TO DENY THE HOLY SPIRIT?
*(By S. Rieley, 25 year lay minister of faith formation)*

From Lumen Gentium Nov 21$^{st}$ 1964 article 32 paragraph 7 Pope Paul VI writes.

*"Upon all the laity, therefore, rests the noble duty of working to extend the divine plan of salvation to all men of each epoch and in every land.* ***Consequently, may every opportunity be given them so that, according to their abilities and the needs of the times, they may zealously participate in the saving work of the church.****"*

We as Laity are called to use the gifts that the Holy Spirit has instituted in us through the Sacraments for the divine plan of Salvation. What a blessing we are. **We** are The Church.

**When we choose to actively participate in the perpetuation of the behaviors that keep the hierarchy on a pedestal, we deny the Holy Spirit**. This places them above scrutiny and thus encourages their transgressions. We as laity often know the truth as the Holy Spirit manifests it in us, but we deny that knowledge and accept mediocrity.

Recently I was employed in the Catholic Church whom I love to the depths of my soul. I discovered that a pastor, upon assignment to a parish can walk in at any time and fire all the staff for no reason, get rid of the sacred art and the cherished music of the people, or do anything else he chooses to do with no accountability. I saw many of my brothers and sisters "let go" just as they neared retirement age, because they were female or because they were not clerics.

I saw many ostracized because they disagreed with "father". I saw many denied the opportunities to share their Gifts with the communities because father did not like "that". I witnessed the ultimate power given to those in charge and experienced those who abused that power as well as those who worked with the Spirit to further the saving work of the Church.

During this ministry I experienced firsthand the workings of the 'Roman' Catholic Cult behaviors. I was working in a parish that was full of life and valued the gifts of the Holy Spirit working not only through the Pastor and the staff but also through the community.

The Bishop decided that this model of church was not to be tolerated and sent in a Pastor to "clean out the "riff raff" and replace it with those who "follow the orders of the Bishop". There was no accountability for the actions of the incoming

Pastor or the Bishop. Those in our community who raised their voices were ignored or silenced.

**Those who believe that the "hierarchy is always right" remained to elevate the Pastor to his polished pedestal while denying the workings of the Spirit in this community**. The Pastor was now placed above scrutiny by the people as well as the Bishop. The light of the Spirit was extinguished.

***"Thus, you will know them by their fruits."*** *(Matt. 7:20)*

We, as laity have a responsibility to uphold the works of the Holy Spirit in our lives and communities, and cease to contribute to the perpetuation of our 'Roman' Catholic Cult.

Amen to the workings of the Spirit. I and so many other faithful Catholics continue to seek community in the Eucharist and in each other as each has been given their gifts. Faith, Hope, and Charity are still alive in our Church. We the laity have a responsibility to our Church, and one of those responsibilities is to hold each other, especially our hierarchy, responsible to the work of the Spirit in the world.

Ephesians 4:1-6 *Therefore I, the prisoner of the Lord, urge you to walk in a manner worthy of the calling with which you have been called, with all humility and gentleness, with patience, bearing with one another in love, being diligent to keep the unity of the Spirit in the bond of peace. There is one body and one Spirit, just as you also were called in one hope of your* calling; *one Lord, one faith, one baptism, one God and Father of all who is over all and through all and in all.*

## WISDOM OF THE HOLY SPIRIT FOR THE CLERGY

- There are lay people in your parish who have the gift of **PREACHING** and are better preachers than maybe you.

- There are lay people in your parish who have been given the gift of **WITNESSING** and have no place in your liturgies to witness to the Holy Spirit and Jesus, which is one of the main ways the Spirit moves like it did at Pentecost.

- There are lay people in your parish who have been given a pronounced gift of **HEALING,** when they pray over or with people, there is an experience of the Holy Spirit healing the person, more than when they are anointed by a priest who simply reads a rote prayer, puts oil on their forehead and palms, then leaves.

- There are lay people who have **WORDS OF KNOWLEDGE** and **PROPHECY**, but also have no place in the parish or liturgies to voice these words from the Lord and have them confirmed by others who have this gift of the Holy Spirit.

- Do the clergy and hierarchy even believe in these gifts of the Holy Spirit? Have they even heard from people who have these gifts?

- There are lay people who have the gift of **DELIVERANCE** as promised by Jesus as signs that will follow **All believers**, not just the Priest.

- There are lay people who have the gift of **DISCERNMENT**, like Peter, knowing the difference between God's word and their personal interpretation, or men's. Do the clergy and hierarchy even understand what the gift of **Discernment** is and how it works according to the early Christians and the Pauline communities, who depended on it to know the Lords Will?

# CHAPTER 4

## A HOLY SPIRIT LED CHURCH LIKE THE EARLY CHRISTIANS WILL BE THE NEW 'REMNANT' CATHOLIC CHURCH

These will be all Christian *(Including Catholics)* denominations that not only experience the Holy Spirit, but also seek and are given the Gifts of the Holy Spirit to lead and minister to one another.

## LEADERSHIP OF THE 'REMNANT'

*(Based on the Pauline Communities)*

**APOSTOLOI:** The Leader of the community who had experienced the Holy Spirit, proclaimed and witnessed to their faith, like Junia, a woman introduced to Peter by St. Paul as an ***'Apostoloi'***. Her gift was to gather, organize, witness to, and lead.

For Paul it did not mean Priest or Bishop, or one of the twelve chosen by Jesus. Paul was not at the last supper, or at Pentecost, but considered himself no less an ***'Apostoloi'***. Why, because he, like them, received the gift of the Holy Spirit to preach, witness, and lead.

**PROPHETS**: They were recognized and appointed by the community because the Lord had gifted them with discernment of the Holy Spirit, knowing the difference between Gods Will, their own, or mans. Their prophecies had to be confirmed by other members who had the gift, to confirm that the Spirit was giving the same message to more than one person.

**TEACHERS**: These were members given the gift of the Holy Spirit to Teach and were also appointed by the community because when they taught and witnessed to their experience of Jesus and the Holy Spirit, those who listened felt the Spirit and the Lord's Truth replace their confusion, not only filling them with theology, but Wisdom and Light to guide them on their journey.

**PRESIDER**: Any of the above who, besides their leadership gifts, manifested the gift to preside at the breaking of the bread would be appointed by the discernment of the Leader, Prophets, as well as the community. Why, because when they said the words of Jesus at the last supper, those present would experience not only the Risen Christ in the Eucharist, but also the love of Lord in the Presider, who pointed his sisters and brothers to focus on Jesus and not the liturgical protocols or rubrics.

**GIFTS OF THE HOLY SPIRIT FOR THE COMMUNITY**

- **PREACHING**
- **WITNESSING**
- **HEALING**
- **MIRACLE WORKERS**
- **DELIVERANCE**
- **WORDS OF KNOWLEDGE**
- **PRAYING IN THE SPIRIT**

**QUESTION:** Do you know a priest or bishop who has all these gifts of the Holy Spirit? If not, why not, if they are supposed to

have them and been appointed by others in the hierarchy who claim that they are the only dispensers of the Holy Spirit and sole possessors of the authority to do so?
Sounds more like a 'Cult' than a faith led by the way Jesus promised:

- *"Wait here. In a few days the Father will send another Advocate, the Holy Spirit, who will teach you ALL things and remind you of everything I taught you." (Jn. 14:26)*

When they asked Jesus how to know what's from the Spirit and what's from man, Jesus answered with the parable of the fig tree that didn't bear fruit. If it doesn't bear fruit, cut it down and throw it away. In other words, it may have worked in the past, but doesn't now, so stop doing it that way.

Since the great outpouring of the Holy Spirit *(A new Pentecost)* at the Second Vatican Council, when the 'People of God- all believers were proclaimed 'the Church', not just the Hierarchy, little by little the 'Roman Hierarchy' took back their power and authority and once again have placed the Holy Spirit under their 'Roman' structure instead of the Gifts of the Holy Spirit given to all believers as the Spirit wishes.

That's why there is a shortage of priests, large numbers of priests who left, and one out of three believers leaving the Catholic Church.

Young couples and children no longer go to church, and most serious and troubling is not the lack of priests, but the lack of ministry for the sick, suffering, dying, and sacraments, especially the Eucharist. Why, because once again the

Sacraments and gifts of the Holy Spirit reside in only one person- the priest.

The 'Roman' Catholic Church has and is becoming a Cult. The 'Roman' Church has lost its Spiritual compass and moral authority, especially with the sex abuse that has permanently damaged millions of children and adults, not just in the past sixty years, but since the 'Roman ' church demanded Celibacy for the clergy.

Jesus never demanded celibacy for his Apostles and Disciples. Why, because it is unnatural and contrary to human nature. It has from the beginning allowed Satan and Evil to tempt and seduce men who were called to be Priests but never wanted to be celibate, forced by the all-male 'Roman' structure of control to simply obey and accept it.

The result is all the sexual immorality in the Papacy, Bishops, and Priests, 'The Roman Catholic Cult of Men'!

Many of the members of the Hierarchy and Clergy have been seduced and corrupted by the appropriation of the Holy Spirit's Power to themselves and have done so without their acknowledging or knowing it, yet continue to bear 'no fruit for their people', or the Church, but only assert their authority. Those infected need to 'Reform' themselves and the Church. As stated before, Power corrupts and absolute Power absolutely corrupts.

**A POSSIBLE REMEDY**: Those infected need a 'Spiritual Enema'. I mean that literally.

I do believe this was the Serpent's temptation in the Garden, the Original Sin. *"Eat of this fruit and you will be like God,"* Isn't this the great Satanic temptation for individuals, people in positions of authority, politicians, governments, movements, political parties, Religions and cults; unbridled power to oppress, control, manipulate, degrade, punish, and marginalize, all with sanctimonious self-righteousness and accountable to no one.

## MISLEADING THE FAITHFUL TO PERPETUATE THE SYSTEM
(**A Pretense** of Religion, but **denying** its power)

### PARABLE OF 'NO FIRE'

There was a man who invented the art of making fire. He took his tools and went to a tribe in the north, where it was bitterly cold. He taught the people there to make fire. He showed them the uses to which they could put fire----they could cook, keep themselves warm, brighten up the darkness. They were so grateful that they learned the art of making fire. But before they could express their gratitude, the man disappeared. He wasn't concerned with getting their recognition or gratitude. He was only concerned with their well-being.

He went to another tribe, where he again began to show them the value of his invention. People were interested there, too, a bit too interested for the peace of mind of their priests, who began to notice that this man was drawing crowds and they were losing their popularity. So they decided to do away with him and put him to death.

But they were afraid now that the people might turn against them, so they had a portrait of the man and mounted it on the main altar of the temple. The instruments for making fire were placed in front of the portrait, and the people were taught to revere the portrait and pay reverence to the instruments of fire, which they did dutifully for centuries. The veneration and worship went on and on, **but there was NO FIRE!**

### Where's the fire?  Where's the love?
This is what Jesus and spirituality are about, but we have been taught and tend to control the Spirit and others, lose it, and create religion instead, don't we?

### CONCLUSION:
- And so, if prayer isn't leading to fire and the experience of God and the Holy Spirit

- If adoration isn't leading to compassion and love

- If the liturgy and mass isn't leading to Jesus

- And if Jesus isn't leading to life and bearing fruit, of what use is religion except to create more division, factions, fanaticism, and antagonism?

**SUMMARY**: Have we been taught to worship liturgy, words, protocols and the priest, instead of the Risen Lord in the Eucharist and having supper with him?

## JESUS POINTS OUT THE EVIL THAT HAS SEDUCED THE RELIGIOUS LEADERS, 2000 YEARS AGO AND TODAY

- *"You tie up heavy loads and put them on men's shoulders, but you yourselves are not willing to lift a finger to help them." (Mt. 23:4)*

- *"Everything they do is done for people to see: They make their phylacteries wide and the tassels on their elaborate garments long" (Mt. 23:5)*

- *"They love the place of honor at banquets and the most important seats in the synagogues." (Mt. 23:6)*

- *"They love to be greeted in the marketplaces and to have men call them 'Rabbi'." (Mt. 23:7)*

- *"Woe to you, teachers of the law and Pharisees, you hypocrites! You are like whitewashed tombs, which look beautiful on the outside, but on the inside full of dead men's bones and all corruption." (Mt. 23:8*

- *"You snakes! You brood of vipers! How will you escape being condemned to hell?" (Mt. 23:33)*

**RESULTS:** Catholics are confused and divided by the disillusionment and loss of trust in the hierarchy and leadership.

# CHAPTER 5

## THE HOLY SPIRIT, OR THE 'ROMAN' CATHOLIC CHURCH IS WASTING ITS TIME

Many Christians, especially Catholics, have never experienced the Holy Spirit and the unconditional love of Jesus. Without judging anyone or the Church, I believe this is true, because in the past no one ever taught us that we could experience the Holy Spirit or even how to. This experience of intimacy with God is missing in a number of the leaders in parish communities.

The most tragic thing is that this is the whole purpose of the coming of Jesus, his life, suffering, death and resurrection. Specifically, this was and is the ultimate goal of God and not my own interpretation. Listen to Jesus' words and prayer, just before his passion and death.

**JESUS:**
*"I am praying not only for these disciples, but also for all who will believe in me through their message.* **I pray that they will all be one, just as you and I are one, as you are in me, Father, and I am in you***. May they be one in us, by the love they have for one another, the world will believe you sent me.*

**I have given them the glory you gave me, so they may be one**, *as we are one. May they experience such perfect oneness that the world will know that you sent me,* **that you love them as much as you love me."** *(Jn. 17:21)*

This intimacy and oneness with God, through Jesus, is God the Holy Spirit. It was God's Unconditional Love for us that was driving Jesus to experience, endure, and overcome the fear of suffering and death.

## SUMMARY:
- Jesus saves us from Evil, by **conquering our fear of Suffering and Death**, and forgives our sins.

- **The Holy Spirit is the restoration of the intimacy with God** that was lost because of Evil and Original Sin.

## PENTECOST: THE DIVINE EMBRACE
*"When the day of Pentecost came, they were all together in one place. Suddenly a sound like the blowing of a violent wind came from Heaven and filled the whole house where they were sitting. They saw what seemed to be tongues of fire that separated and came to rest on each of them. All of them were filled with the Holy Spirit and began to speak in other tongues, as the Spirit enabled them." (Acts 2:1)*

## EXPLAINED IN REAL LIFE TERMS
The followers of Jesus in the upper room at Pentecost felt the unconditional love of God for the first time with and in each other, just as Jesus prayed for in John's gospel, as stated before.

What is this like? It is like the unconditional love of a mother for her child through her embrace. There is peace, comfort, and love. Remember how unbelievably wonderful this was with our mother, grandmother, father, or guardian? When you experience God's unconditional love, there are no words to describe how complete and fulfilled you are. Nothing here on Earth can compare or come close to it.

God not only created us, but he also created us for himself. That is why no thing, person or activity here, while we are in our earthly bodies, can ever satisfy us completely. Only becoming one with God's love will. This is why some Christians, who have experienced the Holy Spirit say they have been "saved," and ask others if they have been saved. What they are saying is, "Have you experienced intimacy with Jesus Christ through the Holy Spirit?"

## A PERSONAL RELATIONSHIP WITH JESUS IS WHAT HE WANTS

**At the last supper Jesus said,** *"I no longer call you my servants, but my **Friends**."*

Intimacy with the Lord is not the end, but just the beginning. It is the beginning of experiencing not only the love of God as a warm fuzzy, moon struck, and a volcanic eruption of passion and joy, but meant to refocus our attention from 'looking out the window' to the world for fulfillment, and focusing instead on who and what we were created for—God.

After we experience the Lord and Baptism of the Holy Spirit, we want to experience and know him more and more. What we are talking about here is establishing a deep personal relationship with Jesus. I want to say it again—a deep and personal relationship with Jesus. Here is where many Christians, especially Catholics, get confused.

Now, don't send me any messages, saying that I am picking on Catholics. I am a Catholic and proud of it. I am just speaking from my general experience where a significant number of

Catholics seem to have mostly a monologue relationship with Jesus. In other words, they are baptized, made their First Penance and Communion, got confirmed, go to mass, say the rosary and recite prayers.

This is good and inspiring but is only a faith relationship based upon a monologue. Those who pray this way do all the talking and seldom listen to Jesus talking to them—to know his Will. Jesus also helps make tough decisions, heals, forgives, and delivers us from fear and worry. The kind of relationship Jesus wants with you and me is a **dialogue**. How do I know this is his Will and not my interpretation or teaching? I'll let Jesus take over and teach you himself.

### JESUS:
*"While you are in the world you will suffer, but don't be afraid, for I am with you until the end of time." (Jn. 16:33)*

*"Come to me all who labor and are heavy burdened, and I will give you rest." (Mt. 11:28)*

*"Who is my mother, father, brothers and sisters? It is the one who hears and does the will of my Father." (Mt. 12:50)*

*"I have come to give life, and life to the fullest." (Jn. 10:10)*
*"I have come to give you joy and make your joy complete." (Jn. 15)*

*"So, do not be afraid or let your hearts be troubled. Trust in God and trust in me." (Jn. 14:1)*

## SUMMARY:
The way the Lord can communicate with us is through an intimate personal relationship. In addition to this, we can feel his presence when we gather with others who have experienced him. At the last supper, Jesus said, "I do not think of you as my servants, but I call you my friends."

**Whoa!** Is Jesus kidding us? You mean to tell me that God, the Creator of the whole ball of wax, you and me included, is our Friend? It's unbelievable, but also wonderful and true.

Jesus is telling us the kind of relationship God wants with us; that is, one of friendship. He is telling us how he wants to be treated. Yea, Yea, Yea, he wants to be acknowledged as our Lord, and rightly so, but also as our 'friend'. In other words, be yourself, trust him, and talk to him as you would your best friend, because he is.

A mother of two teenagers once told me, "It isn't enough to just believe, go to church, receive Communion, say prayers and try to lead a good life. You need to experience Jesus and the Holy Spirit with your kids."

I have heard this millions and millions of times from people—even children to senior citizens, who have felt the awesome love of Jesus for and in them, and how Jesus is transforming their lives?

Through a personal dialogue relationship with Jesus every day, all day, now the Lord can teach you, forgive you, heal you, and help you with your decision-making by a deep awareness that he is actually with you as he said. *("I will be with you every day")*

**Whoa** again! You mean to tell me that I've been dealing with my problems, fears, worries and suffering alone, saying "Help me Lord" prayers and trying to fix them by myself, feeling as if he isn't hearing me and a million miles away?

Being baptized by the Holy Spirit is essential in having a personal relationship with Jesus. This is the way we establish a friendship with anybody. We need to know them first, and that is by spending time with them and experiencing them, not just receiving information about them. The question here that Jesus and I want to answer is what is the Baptism of the Holy Spirit?

## **WHAT IS THE BAPTISM OF THE HOLY SPIRIT?**

- When baptized with the Holy Spirit, you will receive an intimate embrace and experience of the Lord's unconditional love.

- You will experience a new strength and boldness from God, to overcome temptation, Evil, and Sin.

- You will know when you have experienced the Baptism of the Holy Spirit, because it is unlike anything else you have felt with your faith. The apostles at Pentecost experienced the Holy Spirit like a strong driving wind and fire.

**STORY: PETER AND CORNELIUS** *(A Roman Centurion and Gentile)* and his whole household experienced the Holy Spirit and praised the Lord in tongues.

*"Peter went inside and found a large gathering of people. He said to them: You are well aware that it is against our law for a Jew to associate with or visit a Gentile. However, God has shown me that I should not call anyone impure or unclean. Why have you sent for me?*

*Now we are all here in the presence of God to listen to everything the Lord has commanded you, Peter, to tell us. Then Peter began to speak: We are witnesses of everything Jesus did in the country of the Jews and in Jerusalem. They killed him by hanging him on a cross, but God raised him from the dead on the third day and caused him to be seen by us. He commanded us to preach to the people and testify that he is the one whom God appointed as Judge of the living and the dead.*

*While Peter was still speaking these words, the Holy Spirit came on all who heard the message. The circumcised believers who arrived with Peter were astonished that the Holy Spirit was poured out upon the Gentiles, because they heard them speaking in tongues and praising God. Then Peter said, "Surely, no one can stand in the way of their being baptized with water. They have received the Holy Spirit, just as we have. Peter ordered they be baptized with water in the name of Jesus Christ."(Acts 10)*

## THE EXPERIENCE OF THE HOLY SPIRIT

- Your life is changed. God's power often passes through your body like a powerful current and fills you with an infinite joy and happiness.

- The apostles were so full of joy that the people thought they were drunk.

- There is no set timetable for when you experience the Baptism of the Holy Spirit.

How each of us experiences the Holy Spirit differs according to where we are in our relationship with God and Jesus. Some experience the Baptism like the apostles at Pentecost and Cornelius' family, while others more gradually through preachers, teachers, witnesses, and situations.

Others who are filled with the Spirit can be evident just by looking at them. It's like what Jesus said to Nicodemus,

- *"The Spirit is like the Wind. You cannot see it, yet it moves where it will and when it will." (Jn. 14:6)*

Some denominations preach that you are "not saved" unless you experience the Holy Spirit exactly the way they did at Pentecost. As Catholics, we don't believe that is the only way the Spirit moves or saves.

- *"Anyone who believes in their heart and confesses with their lips that Jesus Christ is Lord will be saved." (Rom. 10:9)*

- *"God is love, and anyone who loves, knows God. God is in them and they are in God." (1 Jn. 4:16)*

- *"Enter into the kingdom prepared for you from the beginning of time, for I was hungry, and you gave me something to eat; thirsty and you gave me a drink..." (Mt. 25: 31-40)*

## **WHY DOES THE 'ROMAN' CATHOLIC CHURCH AND CLERGY NEED THE BAPTISM OF THE HOLY SPIRIT?**

- When baptized with the Holy Spirit, you will become bold and unafraid, just as Peter, the Blessed Mother, and Jesus' followers were on the day of Pentecost.

- The Word of God will suddenly become alive for you, and you will experience wisdom and guidance from God's word, especially when you come into difficult situations. You will be less afraid of anyone or anything, not even Evil itself, by living every day for the Lord.

- You will receive gifts of the Holy Spirit, according to the Lord's plan for your life and service: Healing, Preaching, Witnessing boldly, Teaching, Discernment of the Lord's Will, and spiritual works of mercy.

## **TEENS BAPTIZED WITH THE HOLY SPIRIT WITNESS TO THEIR EXPERIENCE**

- "I only wish I experienced Jesus before, when I was a kid. Jesus is great, and he is 'big time' in my life now." *(Jason, Florida)*

- "When I first experienced Jesus, it is hard to describe, because, I mean, he's God and all, but it was incredible. he really loves me and believes in me." *(Maggie, NJ)*

- "A lot of kids at school think it is un-cool to believe in Jesus, go to church, and pray. Boy, are they missing out. I feel sorry for them." *(Jim, NJ)*

- "Now when I go to mass, I'm not bored, because I go to spend time with and talk to Jesus, and many times I can feel him right there, especially when I go to Communion." *(Dan, NH)*

- "I am in a teenage prayer group, and we pray together at youth group. One of my best friends that I have been friends with since the first grade is not in my prayer group. I have been going to the prayer group for only two years, and I feel closer to them than I do with my friend from first grade. I think the reason is we pray and have actually experienced Jesus together." *(Mike, Buffalo, NY)*

- "If I could, I would tell every teenager and adult that Jesus wants them to experience the Holy Spirit and is waiting for them to ask. I have experienced Jesus and have a personal relationship with him now. He's more of a friend now and not like what a lot of people and even I use to do— just go to church, listen to stories about Jesus, and say prayers to him. Now I want to go to church and get involved in ministry and service and live the way Jesus wants me to. The joy and peace I have experienced is greater than anything other kids who don't believe in Jesus have offered me in high school." *(Hannah, NY)*

If all we do is believe, go to church, say prayers, and try to lead a good life, we are missing the **'more'** of why God came in Jesus—the Baptism of the Holy Spirit.

## "THE HOPE FOR THE 'ROMAN' CATHOLIC CHURCH IS THE HOLY SPIRIT, ACCORDING TO POPE FRANCIS

Pope urges German Church to walk together, moved by the Spirit.

In a Letter published June 29, Pope Francis offers his support to the synodal journey of the Church in Germany in which he expresses his appreciation for the German Church, exhorting it not to walk alone and emphasizing the centrality of the Holy Spirit in ecclesial renewal.

*Fr. Bernd Hagenkord SJ - Vatican City*
*"We are all aware that we are living not only in an age of change but also of epochal change that raise new and old questions which call for a justified and necessary debate,"* Pope

Francis writes in his Letter published on Saturday. He says he is aware of the dramatic situation of the Church in the country and offers his support to the reflection on the issue.

### *Journeying together*
The Letter is the Pope's contribution to the synodal journey which the bishops decided upon during their Plenary Assembly in March this year. Together with the representatives of the Central Committee of German Lay Catholics and external experts, the Church wants to discuss the central themes of the crisis.

The starting point for this synodal journey was a study commissioned by the bishops themselves on the theme of sexual abuse by the clergy and consecrated persons, but there are also other issues, such as the aging of communities, the lack of vocations, the non-acceptance of Catholic teaching on sexuality and the lifestyle of priests.

### *Centrality of the Holy Spirit*
Pope Francis does not answer these concrete questions. His contribution is intended to be a spiritual foundation for the debate. He does not offer solutions, he does not forbid discussions, but in the style of "Evangelii Gaudium", the Pope recalls the centrality of the Holy Spirit.

### *Synodality*
In the Letter, the centrality of faith, evangelization and, above all, the Holy Spirit are repeatedly emphasized from various perspectives. Translated into everyday life, the Pope writes, "This stimulates the emergence and continuation of processes

that build us up as God's people, instead of seeking immediate results with premature and 'mediatic' consequences".

## Temptations
"At the basis of this temptation," the Pope warns, "there is the belief that the best response to the many problems and shortcomings that exist, is to reorganize things, change them and 'put them back together' to bring order and make ecclesial life easier by adapting it to the current logic or that of a particular group". **The Pope explains that an organized ecclesial reality solves nothing because it also needs the "bite of the Gospel", its freshness.**

### Evangelization – criterion par excellence
The Pope calls for proceeding wisely. The rational vision of problems has its meaning but this is not the fulfillment of "our faithfulness". The Holy Father returns to his central message: "pastoral conversion". Evangelization, he says, must be the "guiding criterion par excellence".

According to the Pope, the centrality of the Spirit also shapes the way debates are conducted. "The synod vision does not eliminate contradictions or confusion" nor does it subordinate conflicts to false compromises.

"Evangelization lived in this way," observes Pope Francis, "is not a tactic of repositioning the Church in today's world", it is not a "retouching" that adapts the Church to the spirit of the times by making her lose her originality and her prophetic mission. Neither does evangelization mean "an attempt to recover habits and practices that make sense in other cultural contexts": a double rejection of those who seek salvation through adaptation or traditionalism.

## True reform and synodality

"The challenges that await us, the various issues and questions that emerge," the Pope observes, "cannot be ignored or hidden, but must be faced ensuring they are neither entangled nor lost sight of, narrowing our horizons and reality."

This is how the Pope summarizes his vision of the synod path. Everyone, especially the "simple and small", must be heard.

"Let us walk together along the way, as an apostolic body, and listen to each other under the guidance of the Holy Spirit, even if we do not think the same way," the Pope urges adding, "The Lord shows us the way of the Beatitudes".

**"Blessed are those who seek Righteousness, Righteousness shall be theirs."**

# CHAPTER 6

## THE REMNANT: THE SPIRIT-LED CATHOLICS AND BELIEVERS IN THE LAST DAYS:

The systemic corruption in the Catholic hierarchy for centuries has produced opposing factions that has caused extreme confusion and disillusionment among the faithful, as I said earlier. Given the strong probability that the obsession with power will continue to imprison members in the clergy, reform in the near future will mostly likely be a far-fetched dream.

This is discouraging news for the faithful. However, just as Evil shows its Evil head and presence, the power of the heavens is opened and the Holy Spirit pours the unconditional love of God into people's hearts and makes all things new. This has been the history of our salvation since the beginning.

What, where, when, and how will the Holy Spirit dispel the evil that has infected our church. In other words, what do we do in the meantime if the hierarchy does not reform and change?

## GOD'S ANSWER:

*"I ask, then, has God rejected his people? Of course not, for I too am an Israelite, a descendant of Abraham from the tribe of Benjamin. God has not rejected his people who he foreknew. Do you not know what the scripture says about Elijah, how he pleads with God against Israel?*

*Lord, they have killed your prophets, they have torn down your altars, and I alone am left, and they are seeking my life."* But *what is God's response to him. I have left for myself seven thousand who have not knelt before Satan. So also at the time there is a **REMNANT, chosen by Grace, not by works of men whose hearts were hardened.**" (Rom. 11:1-6)*

Are you chosen by the Lord to join in the **New Remnant** for this age, as the 'Roman' Catholic Church deteriorates into a cult-like religion, losing its moral and spiritual authority, led by men who have co-opted the sole dissemination of the Holy Spirit to themselves?

Because of the 'Roman' political structure, many are and will continue to be without the gifts to impart the Lord's love, wisdom, and healing. Evil's power will render them as blind guides and expose them as the new Pharisees, who make their laws equal to God's commandments.

- *"You make man made laws equal to God's commandments." (Mt. 23)*

- *"Woe to you teachers of the law and Pharisees, you hypocrites! You shut the kingdom of heaven in men's faces. You do not enter, nor do you let those enter who are trying." (Mt. 23)*

# THE NEW CATHOLIC CHURCH OF THE HOLY SPIRIT

## WHO ARE AND WILL THEY BE?

- All baptized with the Holy Spirit, specifically those who have experienced the unconditional love, power, and wisdom of the Holy Spirit and have a daily personal dialogue relationship with Jesus as their teacher, guide, and Lord

- Those who experience Jesus and the Holy Spirit with others, who have and experience a spiritual bond with one another as they feel the Lord's presence in and with each other

- People who experience the Holy Spirit when they gather together, making them one family, as Jesus prayed for

- People who seek the gifts of the Holy Spirit and given them for themselves, their community and others

## THE GIFTS OF LEADERSHIP FOR SPIRIT-LED CATHOLICS

**APOSTLES:** They are to Lead and discern the Holy *Spirit (What's from man and what's from God)*, not just common sense, a democratic vote, a personal idea, or what's practical. It is a gift whereby the Holy Spirit directly reveals the Truth to the person who has been given the gift to recognize it.

**PROPHETS**: They have the gift to discern what is from the Lord and what is not, confirmed by others with the gift.

**TEACHERS**: They have the gift to speak and teach the Truths of God, and when they do, believers are drawn to it by the power of the Spirit who Jesus said will "Teach you all things".

## GIFTS OF THE HOLY SPIRIT FOR INDIVIDUALS IN THE COMMUNITY FOR THEIR SISTERS AND BROTHERS

- **HEALERS**
- **PREACHERS**
- **MIRACLE WORKERS**
- **PRESIDERS**
- **DELIVERANCE**
- **WORDS OF KNOWLEDGE**
- **PRAYING IN THE SPIRIT**

*"Many gifts, one Spirit"*

## THE CATHOLIC FAITH OF THE REMNANT

If you are disappointed, disillusioned, and not being spiritually fed by the 'Roman' Catholic Church or your parish. If you have a gift or gifts of the Holy Spirit, but are not recognized by your Pastor and find no place in your parish to use them, then the **Remnant spirituality** is for you, as promised by God and the words of the New Testament.

- Refocus your faith and love on the Lord instead of the Church and ask to be baptized with the Holy Spirit, i.e. to actually experience, feel, and become one with the Lord's unconditional Love for you, not just believing in him, but being embraced by him. Keep asking until you do. When the Lord knows you are ready and really trusting him by your perseverance, you will. Hallelujah!

- Keep practicing your Catholicism and wonderful catholic traditions and spirituality as listed below. Be open to all the beautiful traditions and prayer forms that make us unique and rich in the ways to walk with Jesus. **WHAT ARE THEY?**

## THE CATHOLICISM OF THE REMNANT'

**YOU CATHOLICS ARE A BIT STRANGE & A TAD CRAZY**
(From the words of a Non-Catholic onlooker)

- **You Catholics have prayer cards, pictures, statues, and medals.** You say they help remind and help you to be aware of the lord is with you and loves you.

- **You get fresh palm leaves just before Easter and make crosses and other religious symbols** out of them; then, a year later, you burn them and on a certain Wednesday. You put their ashes on your foreheads and walk around in public letting everyone know you are sinners...and doing penance for your sins.

- **You have this string of different size beads**, tied together with a cross at one end. You repeat the same prayer over and over, to a woman named Mary, whom you claim gave birth to God, while still a virgin. You call her the mother of god, and you call the beads, the rosary, and believe this prayer leads you closer to God.

- **You bless water** and you believe that god will protect you, if you make the sign of the cross on your forehead with it, because it reminds you that he is with you.

- **You sprinkle this water on almost anything**—dogs, cats, horses, fish, rabbits, trucks, cars, boats, even children's stuffed animals and say that this makes them blessed and special not only to you but to God.

- **You light different colored candles** and place them in front of pictures, icons, and statues for specific reasons, needs, requests, trusting that the God will answer and be with you.

- **You don't believe in ghosts**; nevertheless, you ask favors of people who have died; yet, because you believe they are not dead, but alive with god in heaven, they can intercede for you and inspire you.

- **You confess your sins to another human being** and believe that this human being's forgiveness is God's forgiveness, and is also the forgiveness of your church family, and all at the same time.

- **You love ritual, imagery, statues and pictures that remind you of holy people**, who have gone before you that you claim to experience the mystery of God's presence and love in and through them.

- **You say that you receive Jesus as your food and drink**; through something that looks like, feels like, tastes like bread and wine, but it isn't. —you say it really is the body and blood and unconditional love of the risen Lord who said he would never abandon you, your risen Christ in the Eucharist, not just a memory of the last supper 2000 years ago, but really him, in a unique and loving way.

- **What's really strange is while the world is having happy hours, you're making holy hours** spending time sitting in front of a brass box you call a tabernacle, where you say your risen Jesus lives in that bread, but you say, that by the end of the hour, no matter what your worried about, or what your problems are, that being with Jesus gives you peace of mind that nobody and nothing else does. I don't see any other Christian churches doing this, only you 'Catholics'.

- **Then I watch you not only loving God, but loving one another**, even though you are sinners, like everyone else, claiming that this is what Jesus asks you to do, that the 'Catholic church' is not a museum of saints, but a hospital for sinners.

- **You Catholics are really strange, but I must admit and say, that all these things you do that make you 'Catholic' and unique, make me wonder, if I am missing out on something wonderful, from God.**

# HOORAY FOR CATHOLICISM!

## HOW TO CREATE AND CONNECT WITH THE 'REMNANT' CATHOLIC CHURCH

- Join women's, men's, or mixed prayer groups whose purpose is to 'experience' the Holy Spirit, grow closer to the Lord, discern his Will and share ways to do it, heal, support, and become sisters and brothers who love one another.

- If there are none in your parish or area, then seek out a Christian church that has scripture and prayer groups that are led by the Holy Spirit with the gifts for healing, witnessing, and teaching. Make sure they are not anti-Catholic nor anti other Christian denominations or condemn other Religions.

- Ask family members, friends, and neighbors who are Catholic and other Christians if they would like to start and join together in each other's homes to pray together. Whether you join or start a group then ask the Holy Spirit to give members the gifts of the Spirit to heal, teach, deliver, and lead.

**JESUS SAID**:
"These are the signs that will follow **ALL BELIEVERS**, (Not just the Priests). "Those upon who they will lay their hands will be healed... in my Name they will cast out demons."
(Mk. 16:17-18)

- The point here is that Jesus said **ALL** believers may be given these gifts. The 'Roman' Catholic Church denied the Holy Spirit to all believers by teaching that only the Priest has these powers. **NOT TRUE!**

- The Eucharist, the presence of the Risen Christ, the unconditional love of God with us, is central to our Catholic faith. The Eucharist is the Lord's way of being with us who said he would never abandon us. To receive and experience the Lord with and in you, go to mass and spend time making holy hours before the Eucharist. Just remember when you finish, don't leave him there. Take and be aware that he is with you as he said and continue to discern where he is leading you.

- When forming your conscience, making decisions, and discerning what's right, wrong, and the Lord's will, listen to what the Catholic Church teaches, especially on matters of morality and justice. They represent centuries of truths that are absolute, those that are constant, and those that are evolving. They are one of the greatest gifts that the Catholic Church has given, not only to believers but the whole world.

- There are those teachings that are more absolute than others. For example the absolute and never changing truth of our faith and Catholicism is the 'Creed'. It is what makes us Catholics and receivers of Divine revelation.

- There are those teachings that are moral absolutes, like abortion and respect for life.

- There are the lesser moral teachings, like birth control and areas that may change with time.

- There are the rich proclamations, encyclicals, and teachings of the Church that are profound truths to guide believers in their decisions and help form their conscience.

Given all the politicization of the 'Roman' Church and the corruption throughout its history, consider a good warning from Jesus.

*"Listen to what they say, but do <u>NOT</u> imitate them."*

# CHAPTER 7

# THE CATHOLIC REMNANT'S ATTITUDE TOWARD THE 'ROMAN' CATHOLIC CHURCH

## Based on St. Francis' attitude toward the Roman Catholic Church and Clergy

- Pray for them, the Pope, Bishops, and Priests.

- Pray for those in the Hierarchy that 'Get it' and are led by the Holy Spirit, yet are controlled by the man-made policies and laws of their superiors who don't 'get it' and have been seduced by power and self-righteousness.

- Pray for the spirit-filled Priests who are frustrated by all they know the Holy Spirit can and wants to do, but are prevented from doing so by fear of reprisal or being suspended and marginalized.

- Do not judge them. That is for God to determine who goes to heaven or hell.

- Forgive them as Jesus teaches all of us to do in the 'Our Father'.

- When given the opportunity, in a peaceful manor, challenge them with the truth, grounded in both the words of Jesus and in our Christian tradition of 2000 years. (*Ex. The early Christians way of life based on the experience and gifts of the Holy Spirit*)

- Be unafraid to challenge the 'Roman' Catholic hierarchy who created these institutional structures of leadership, authority, and ministries that are responsible for the corruption and suffering they have caused to not only believers, but to civilization.

- Don't worry about the **'Roman'** Catholic Church. Those who created the system and perpetuated it let them fix it. Until they have a new Pentecost like the Lord proclaimed at Vatican II, they will continue to reduce the 'Roman' Catholic Church and their followers into a small manageable cult, to sustain their power and position.

- Keep your focus on being a member of the **Remnant** that God promised, a people led by the true Vicar of Christ, the Holy Spirit.

*"The Advocate, the Holy Spirit, whom the Father will send in my name, will teach you **ALL** things and will remind you of everything I have told you." (Jn. 14:16)*

- Listen to what the 'Roman' Church and the clergy have to say, but ask the Holy Spirit and those who have been given the gifts of discernment to know what is from man and what is from the Spirit, trusting what Jesus said,

    *"You have only one teacher." (Mt. 23:10)*

- The Remnant must read, listen, and share the scripture, especially what Jesus said, taught, and did. The Remnant must also more and more learn to have a personal **dialogue** relationship with Jesus and learn how and the ways he reveals his Will to you. The more you learn and live this way, the more you will be able to know what is of the Spirit and what is not.

- Jesus was asked this, and this is what he said and is of the utmost importance to read it again. Why, because this is the stumbling block for the Hierarchy to see and do, and so they remain blind and in denial.

*"If the fig tree does not bear fruit, **cut it down**."* (Lk. 13:9)

In other words, if what you or the church is doing does not bear fruit, **stop doing it that way**.

**EXAMPLE**: For the past sixty years the Pope, Bishops, Priests, and Pastors have been asking us to join them in asking for more vocations to the Priesthood. Has their prayers been answered? I think not, and as a matter of fact vocations have and continue to decrease dramatically.

Has anyone dared to question their supposedly having the gift of discerning God's will? Are they deaf or just asking to cement and solidify their power and authority as in the past?

Put simply, according to Jesus as to what's from the Holy Spirit, God has been telling the hierarchy that their job description of

Priesthood has and no longer is bearing fruit for the past sixty years. Maybe, just maybe, his Will is to **STOP** doing it this way. At Vatican II, the Lord blessed the Church and the world with a new Pentecost and release of the Holy Spirit. The Holy Spirit also revealed that the Church is **'the people of God'**, believers who would recognize and experience the new outpouring of the Holy Spirit.

### DID IT HAPPEN, YES!

1. The Charismatic Renewal and movement with the people forming groups and given the many gifts of the Holy Spirit to lead, teach, heal, witness, and discern

2. Charismatic Masses where believers were able to manifest their gifts of the Spirit to praise the Lord throughout the mass, culminating in their reception of the Risen Lord and his unconditional Love.

3. Worldwide Cursillo movement and spirituality centered on experiencing the Holy Spirit, led by lay people

4. Groups that followed the Holy Spirit and those given the obvious and powerful gifts of the Spirit that bear fruit

5. Healing services with people having the gift of healing, laying hands on and praying over their brothers and sisters

6. Many shared prayer groups, men's and women's groups, international groups, teen groups, and flourishing evangelical groups led by the experience of the Holy Spirit as promised

7. Believers and non-believers being baptized with the Holy Spirit, resting in the spirit like St. Paul

8. National men's and women's Christian conferences and retreats to experience the Holy Spirit

9. The rise of televangelists and denominations centered of experiencing the Holy Spirit and manifesting the charismatic gifts of the Spirit

What happened to all these outpourings of the Holy Spirit? Well you guessed it, because they challenged and threatened the authority and power of the clergy, they were down played, openly rejected, ridiculed, and relegated to maybe the basement of churches. The clergy did not encourage, promote, or assimilate these gifts of the Holy Spirit into the liturgy and sacraments of the 'Roman' Church.

In short, the 'Roman' Church chose not to acknowledge that the Holy Spirit was granting the gifts of the Holy Spirit to others and not solely to them. The "Blind Guides", as Jesus called them have been seduced for centuries by money, power, and sex!

Granted there are good and holy men, but the point here is that the 'Roman' system and structure has been and is corrupt and been seduced by evil, with no checks, balances, or accountability to anyone except themselves. These are the specifics that need major 'Reform' as St. Francis hoped for.

## EXAMPLE #1   **SEX**

*The Vatican on Tuesday released a much-anticipated report about Theodore McCarrick, a former cardinal and archbishop of Washington who was defrocked after allegations of sexual misconduct with adults and minors. Here's what you need to know:*

### Who is Theodore McCarrick?
*McCarrick was one of the most popular and well-known leaders in the U.S. Catholic Church until June 2018, when the then-87-year-old cardinal was suspended for allegedly sexually fondling an altar boy decades earlier. McCarrick, who grew up poor in New York's Washington Heights neighborhood, went on to become a friend and confidant of presidents, prime ministers, professional athletes and other celebrities and was known publicly as a tireless peacemaker, a fundraiser for many Catholic causes and an epic schmoozer.*

*Starting as early as the 1990s, the report confirms, quiet complaints of McCarrick's inappropriate sexual behavior began traveling all the way to the Vatican, yet he continued to rise to lead dioceses in New Jersey — in Metuchen and Newark — and then D.C., where he was made a cardinal. McCarrick was suspended in 2018, then in 2019 became the first-ever cardinal laicized for sexual misconduct with youths and adults.*

### What is the "McCarrick report"?
*In the weeks after McCarrick's June 2018 suspension, multiple other accusations against him surfaced, as well as revelations that there had been complaints to the church hierarchy over the years along with legal settlements between victims and*

three New Jersey dioceses. The Vatican press office in October 2018 put out a **statement** saying that Pope Francis was "concerned by the confusion" among Catholics about what really happened. It said there would be a "thorough study" of all documents accessible to the Vatican "in order to ascertain all the relevant facts, to place them in their historical context and to evaluate them objectively." The report, titled "Report on the Holy See's Institutional Knowledge and Decision-Making Related to Former Cardinal Theodore Edgar McCarrick (1930 to 2017)," was overseen by the Vatican's secretary of state.

Rumors and accusations of who knew what, and when, have flown since 2018, dividing an already polarized church and many Catholics hope the detail the report offers will clarify the truth. Experts say the report is the most extensive public investigation the church has done into a cleric of McCarrick's stature. (By **Michelle Boorstein**, Religious Reporter)

## What the report says about the Popes:
The report says Popes John Paul II, Benedict and Francis were aware of allegations McCarrick may have acted inappropriately with young men. Initially, John Paul decided not to elevate McCarrick to lead dioceses in Chicago, New York City or D.C. — then in 2000 changed his mind after McCarrick wrote to the pope's personal secretary asserting he had never had sexual relations with anyone. Several U.S. bishops also told him that McCarrick had shared a bed with young men but did not indicate with certainty that he had engaged in sexual misconduct.

"This inaccurate information appears likely to have impacted the conclusions of John Paul II's advisers and, consequently, of John Paul II himself," the report said. Under Benedict, the Vatican, acting on new details from a priest, requested McCarrick's give up his position as archbishop of Washington in 2006, after he reached the standard retirement age of 75. Benedict's staff proposed launching a fact-finding mission but the pope opted instead for McCarrick to keep a lower profile — which McCarrick largely ignored. Francis assumed the allegations were false because John Paul would not have permitted "a rotten candidacy to move forward," and responded quickly once a credible allegation that McCarrick abused a minor surfaced.

**Has anyone until now been held accountable?**
Not nearly enough say some victims and their advocates. In August 2018, a former Vatican ambassador dropped a bombshell letter listing a slew of high-ranking church officials in the U.S. and Rome who knew about allegations against McCarrick. The report said many of the people named in the letter did know about allegations against McCarrick, but nobody but McCarrick has been held accountable so far.
The case rocked the Archdiocese of Washington, where his successor, Cardinal Donald Wuerl, retired in **October 2018,** before he had planned to, amid controversy over his handling of abuse cases when he was bishop of Pittsburgh. In January 2019, after denying repeatedly that he'd known anything before June 2018 about sexual misconduct allegations against McCarrick

**The Post reported** that Wuerl had known about an allegation of inappropriate behavior and had reported it to the Vatican in

*2004. Some believe the report lets Pope Francis off too easily. Anne Barrett Doyle, co-director of Bishop*

*Accountability, a group that gathers information on clergy abuse, said Francis's "lack of curiosity" about the allegations against McCarrick "was at best negligent, at worst corrupt." She said the report shows why Church leadership can't self-police. "Accountability won't happen without external oversight."*

## EXAMPLE #2   **MONEY**

*By Nicole Winfield, Associated Press, December 28, 2020*

***ROME*** *-- Pope Francis has formally stripped the Vatican secretariat of state of its financial assets and real estate holdings following its bungled management of hundreds of millions of euros in donations and investments that are now the subject of a corruption investigation.*

*The changes are a response to a spiraling Vatican criminal investigation into years-long allegations of mismanagement of donations and investments by the Vatican's secretariat of state which has resulted in losses of tens of millions of euros at a time of financial crisis for the Holy See.*

*Francis moved against his own secretariat of state amid an 18-month investigation by Vatican prosecutors into the office's 350-million-euro investment into a luxury residential building in London's Chelsea neighborhood and other speculative funds.*

*Prosecutors have accused several officials in the department of abusing their authority for their involvement in the deal, as well several Italian middlemen of allegedly fleecing the Vatican of tens of millions of euros in fees.*

*The scandal has exposed the incompetence of the Vatican's monsignors in managing money, since they signed away voting shares in the deal and agreed to pay exorbitant fees to Italians who were known in business circles for their shady dealings.*

## EXAMPLE #3  POWER

Pope Francis' Address to Pontifical Representatives and Apostolic Nuncios, ZENIT, retrieved June 9, 2017

Addressing apostolic nuncios, who recommend to the pope good candidates for episcopal appointment, Pope Francis said:

*"In the delicate task of carrying out inquiries for episcopal appointments, be careful that the candidates are pastors close to the people, fathers and brothers, that they are gentle, patient and merciful; animated by inner poverty, the freedom of the Lord and also by outward simplicity and austerity of life, that they do not have the psychology of "Princes".*

*Pope Francis wants "a church based not on fancy vestments and infallible pronouncements, but on love of God and love of others." He is critical of a church that is preoccupied with small-minded rules and is a museum for the saintly few rather than, with missionary zeal, being a place of welcome for the many.*

*He has castigated and taken action against clerics whom he sees as living a princely life.* **Francis said clergy should be** *shepherds looking after the people, but knows they can be tempted and corrupted by power.* When they take from the people instead of giving, simony and other corruption can follow. Love between the clergy and people are destroyed.

Francis fears some clerics "become wolves and not shepherds; ... careerism and the search for a promotion [to the hierarchy] come under the category of spiritual worldliness," deceitfully trying to appear holy.

What if Jesus has been asking the leadership and clergy, since Vatican II, to trust him; to step out of their 'comfort' zone and **just do it, like St. Francis?**

### "I NOW AM BORN AGAIN"

- *"What good is it to inherit the whole world and lose your very Soul? (Mt. 16:26)*

- *"There is one thing more you must do. Sell everything you have, give the money to the poor, and then come back and follow me." (Mt. 19:21)*

- *"The gifts you have been given, give them freely to those who have none." (Mt. 10:1-8)*

- *"You cannot serve God and Money. You will love the one and hate the other. You will serve one and despise the other." (Mt. 6:24)*

- *"If anyone of you would be my disciple, you must deny yourself, pick up your cross, and follow me." (Lk. 9:23)*

- *[28] "Why do you worry about clothes and what you wear? See how the lilies of the field grow. They do not labor or spin. [29] Yet I tell you, that not even Solomon in all his splendor was dressed like one of these. [30] If that is how God clothes the grass of the field, which is here today and tomorrow is thrown into the fire, will he not much more clothe you—you of little faith? [31] So do not worry, saying, 'What shall we eat?' or 'What shall we drink?' or 'What shall we wear?' [32] For the pagans and unbelievers run after all these things, and your heavenly Father knows what you need. [33] But seek first his kingdom and his righteousness, and all these things will be given to you as well."*

*(Mt. 6:28)*

## **TO MY BROTHER PRIESTS AND HIERARCHY OF THE CHURCH**

The above is not an attack on the Pope, Bishops, or Priests, but a challenge to reflect on the wealth and externals of our Catholic faith, our rich liturgical accessories, and even our ornate embroidered clerical clothing.

As quoted earlier, Pope Francis said he wants

- *"A church based not on fancy vestments and infallible pronouncements, but on love of God and love of others." He is critical of a church that is preoccupied with small-minded rules and is a museum for the saintly few rather than, with missionary zeal, being a place of welcome for the many.*
- *"A clergy to be shepherds looking after the people, but knows they can be tempted and corrupted by power when they take from the people instead of giving, simony and other corruption can follow, love between the clergy and the people is destroyed.*

Did the apostles and holy women wear rich attire to bring attention to themselves and their service to the Lord? Unlike most other Christian denominations, why do the 'Roman' Catholic clergy and hierarchy think that their vestments inspire people to experience the **poor naked crucified Lord and the Risen Christ in the Eucharist**?

If they really believe this, they do not. For many, they are the clergy's way of enhancing themselves and projecting their clerical authority, **rendering priests unapproachable and separating themselves from the very people they are called to serve and be a brother to**.

To do Jesus Will, he said, *"If anyone of you would be my disciple, you must deny yourself, pick up your cross, and follow me." This* requires the hierarchy **let go** and **Trust** in him; the

**Trust** they promised and committed their life to when they laid prostrate on the floor before they were ordained.

Pope Francis said in an interview about the riches of the Church,

- *"If a believer speaks about poverty or the homeless and leads the life of a pharaoh – this cannot be done,"* he said. *"The Church must speak the truth and **also with witness: the witness of poverty.**"*

Can it be done? Is it possible for the 'Roman' Catholic Church to **reform** and be **changed** radically by the Holy Spirit?

**Yes**, St. Francis did it, so can the Pope, Bishops, Priests, and Clergy. If not, at least choose to try. It's called **TRUST!**

*"Francesco, my Church is in ruins, rebuild it!"*

## EXAMPLE #4  **HEDONISM**

*¹⁹ Now the works of the flesh are evident: sexual immorality, impurity, sensuality, ²⁰ idolatry, sorcery, enmity, strife, jealousy, fits of anger, rivalries, dissensions, divisions, envy, drunkenness, orgies, and things like these. I warn you, as I warned you before, that those who do such things* **will not inherit the kingdom of God.**  (Galatians 5:19-21)

## VATICAN COPS BUST DRUG-FUELED GAY ORGY AT HOME OF CARDINAL'S AIDE

By Tamar Lapin, July 5, 2017

*Vatican police raided a drug-fueled gay-sex party at an apartment belonging to an aide of one of Pope Francis' key advisers, according to a new report.*

*The Holy Father is "enraged," since the home, inhabited by Francesco Cardinal Coccopalmerio's secretary, belongs to the Vatican's Congregation for the Doctrine of Faith — the arm charged with tackling clerical sex abuse, the Italian paper Il Fatto Quotidiano reported.*

*Cops raided the apartment in late June after neighbors voiced concern about multiple people acting strangely while streaming in and out of the residence, the newspaper reported Wednesday.*

*Once police were inside the apartment, they said they found multiple men engaged in rampant drug use and homosexual activity.*

They then arrested the priest — an aide to one of Pope Francis' key advisers — after taking him to a clinic to detox from the drugs he'd ingested.

The unnamed aide is now on a spiritual retreat in a convent in Italy, the paper said.

The aide's apartment building is the same place where Joseph Cardinal Ratzinger lived for about 25 years before becoming Pope Benedict XVI.

Fatto Quotidiano described the building as "a perfect location to enjoy the extraterritorial rights [of the Vatican] without having to undergo neither the checks of the Italian State nor those of the Vatican City."

Pope Francis "has decided to accelerate the retirement" of Coccopalmerio, who serves as president of the Vatican's Pontifical Council for Legislative Texts, the paper said.

Coccopalmerio had recommended the secretary for a promotion to bishop — but his prospects aren't looking good following this incident and two previous alleged drug overdoses, according to an International Business Times report.

"He had proposed his secretary to the episcopate. Fortune that they have not appointed him bishop. Now what would happen?" Il Fatto Quotidiano said. "Someone stopped this appointment before it was too late."

The scandal comes just a week after the Vatican was rocked by sex-abuse allegations against high-ranking church official George Cardinal Pell.

*Pell was charged with multiple counts of historical sexual assault offenses by Australian police.*

*The cardinal, who served as Pope Francis' chief financial adviser and is Australia's most senior Catholic, is the highest-ranking Vatican official ever to be charged in the church's sexual- abuse scandals.*

**FACT**: This is not only the tip of the iceberg, but the tip of the Arctic continent.

**ADD**: Those seduced by Satan, Demons, and Spirits, who submitted to the Power, Money, Sex, and Hedonism (Pleasure), became obsessed, and then possessed to different degrees, becoming **Luciferians** and the new **Illuminati.**

## ... DELIVER US FROM EVIL!

*"Jesus, in your **Name** and by the **Blood** you shed for us on the cross, through the intercession of the Blessed Mother and St. Michael the Archangel, **Bind** and **Cast Out** Satan and all Evil from our Catholic family."*

# CLERICALISM

("Pope: Warns that Poorly Trained Priests Can Become 'Little Monsters'". America Magazine 4, January 2014. Retrieved 9, June 2017)

Pope Francis said of clerical vanity:

*"Look at the peacock; it's beautiful if you look at it from the front. But if you look at it from behind, you discover the truth. ...Whoever gives in to such self-absorbed vanity has huge misery hiding inside them.* **He admonished 138 newly appointed bishops not to surround themselves with "courtiers, climbers, and yes-men"** *but to bring people the Gospel that makes people free.*

Speaking to 120 superiors of religious orders, Francis kept up his campaign against clericalism, saying that seminary formation must be *"a work of art, not a police action"* where seminarians *"grit their teeth, try not to make mistakes, follow the rules smiling a lot, just waiting for the day when they are told 'Good, you have finished formation.'* ...**This is hypocrisy that is the result of clericalism, which is one of the worst evils."** Priestly formation **"must form their hearts. Otherwise we are creating little monsters. And then these little monsters mold the people of God.** *This really gives me goose bumps."*

What Jesus said to chastise the Pharisees *(Priests)* is the same as what he would say to the 'Roman' Catholic Hierarchy and Priesthood today.

- *"Blind guides, you brood of vipers and snakes. You are all clean and righteous on the outside, but inside you are filled with dead men's bones and all corruption."* (Mt. 23:33)

- *"You will not see me here again, not until you learn to say, blessed is he who comes in the name of the Lord."* (Mt. 23:39)

I wonder if this last admonishment of Jesus is why it appears that the Holy Spirit seems to have abandoned the 'Roman' Church's hierarchy and structure of Priestly authority and control.

I also wonder if this is why believers baptized by the Holy Spirit are leaving in droves to follow the Spirit instead of the 'Roman' Catholic Church and practice their Catholic faith in evangelical communities.

One of my intentions in writing this book is to inform Priests and Bishops that the faithful go to Mass to experience and receive the Lord in the Eucharist and to be with other like-minded brothers and sisters. They attend mass, **NOT** to listen to the Priest preach, recite prayers, or worship the rubrics or liturgy, but to be with and receive the Risen Christ and be with their brothers and sisters for fellowship.

- *"They went to the temple every day for the prayers and broke the bread in their homes. And the place where they prayed shook, because they were all filled with the Holy Spirit."* (Acts 2:42)

When was the last time you went to Mass and the Church shook? If it did shake it wasn't because of the Priest, the liturgy, or the way they prayed, but because they experienced the unconditional love and intimacy of the Holy Spirit with and in each other.

And so, I wonder why many of the sacraments that can only be performed by the Priest, don't communicate the Holy Spirit to those who receive them.

**MAYBE HERE'S THE PROOF**:

- Nine out of ten teens being confirmed don't go to church, don't experience the Holy Spirit, and continue to not attend church after they are confirmed. So much for the Bishop as the sole instrument of confirmation and the Holy Spirit. Maybe they need to ask themselves why not, instead of blaming parents and the teenagers.

- First communion classes are smaller and smaller with many of the children's parents not attending mass and after their child receives first communion, they still don't attend. Why is this if the Priest is the sole source of experiencing the Holy Spirit?

- Why are more and more people, especially children, teens, and the young bored when they go to Mass? Could it be that the 'Roman' Priesthood has reduced the Lords supper to a theatrical production with the Priest having the lead role, to be observed and listened to, with only token rote responses from the faithful in the pews.

The numbers of people leaving the 'Roman' Church and not attending Mass may be an indication that the so called liturgical experts are blinded by their obsession with rubrics, wording, grammar, and 'power'. A wakeup call to them and the 'Roman' Priesthood is that when believers go to Mass, they don't worship the Liturgy. They worship the Lord Jesus Christ and want only to receive him in the Eucharist together with their brothers and sisters

The Acts of the Apostles tells us that they broke **bread in their homes**. My questions are:

- Who broke the bread?

- Who appointed them to be the one who broke the bread, reciting the words of Jesus?

- Who broke the bread in the Pauline communities and who appointed them? Did Peter and the Apostles appoint them because they were the first 'Bishops'?

St. Paul wasn't at the last supper and therefore not commissioned and ordained a Priest to consecrate the bread. He was not one of the twelve apostles and therefore not a Bishop. He also was not in the upper room and did not experience the Holy Spirit at Pentecost. So, who gave him the authority to preach, anoint, heal, and baptize with the Holy Spirit? Who appointed those in his communities of believers to break the bread?

**The answer is simple**, the Holy Spirit appointed the person/s to break the bread, by giving them the gift that manifested itself when they presided by simply proclaiming the words of Jesus.

My question to the 'Roman' Church is to answer the above questions regarding St. Paul's ministries, and how the presiders at the breaking of the bread were appointed.

A wake up call is that the person, who broke the bread, was appointed by the Holy Spirit through the community, not by one person. The person who broke the bread was only one of the gifts and ministries of the Holy Spirit, Presider *(Priest)*, equal to all the other ministries and gifts given to believers.

The Hierarchy has fed believers with not totally true teachings, like Jesus ordained those at the last supper to the Priesthood to be the sole presiders at the Eucharist. Also, that as Apostles, they were ordained as Bishops and given sole absolute authority and power over believers with no checks, balances, or accountability. The point here is what is the definition of 'Apostle'?

According to Webster's Dictionary and most likely St. Paul:
**APOSTLE:** *The Greek word* **'Apostoloi'** *means Messenger, True believer, Promoter, Herald, Preacher and Advocate, a person who actively supports or favors a cause.*

**SUMMARY:** The 'Roman' hierarchy for centuries has defined the word <u>Apostle</u> to be a **political and church position** as a 'Bishop', who has the sole authority in matters of faith, teaching, what are valid and illicit practices. They also have appropriated to themselves sole authority to perpetuate that authority and power to others who only they can appoint, *(sounds like an elite men's club to me)*, regardless if they have the gifts of the Holy Spirit or not. No wonder why the 'Roman' Catholic Church is in the mess it is.

Catholicism, as the tradition and practices of the early Christians handed down to us is truly from the Holy Spirit and is unique from all other Christian traditions. The problem is that the Roman influence and system of Leadership and Priesthood have been and continues to be corrupt.

I personally believe that the sex abuse, cover ups, and corruption are being exposed by the media, press, victims, and secular authorities and represent the Lord's way of cleansing and delivering his church from evil people, false teachings, and practices that have not only caused devastating suffering, but have violated and denied the power of God, the Holy Spirit.

- *...In the last days.. They will make a **pretense** of religion and deny its power." (II Tim. 3:5)*

I wonder if this is also a warning of Jesus that they are on the brink of committing the 'unforgiveable' sin.

- *"All manner of **sin** and **blasphemy** shall be forgiven unto men; but the **blasphemy against the Holy Spirit** shall not be forgiven unto men" (Mt. 12:31)*

This is why we all need, including me, to pray for the 'Roman' Catholic Church's leadership, not judge them as to whether they are going to heaven or hell, rather that the Lord and the Father 'deliver them for their blindness and evil' with the Truth- the Holy Spirit that Jesus said will teach them all things and remind them of everything that he said and taught.

- *"You know how the Pharisees and Scribes Lord their authority over the people. It cannot be that way with you." (Mt. 5:20)*

# CHAPTER 8

## 'ROMAN' PRIESTHOOD VS COMMON SENSE

**RP**: *Roman Priesthood*
**CS**: *Common Sense*


**RP**: Only a Priest can minister and disseminate the Holy Spirit to a serious ill or dying person by anointing them with oil.

**CS:** Jesus said, *"These are the signs that will follow **ALL** believers... those upon who they lay their hands will be healed."*

The seriously ill person is not as important to the Lord as the power and authority of the Roman Priesthood. This is insane.

**Example**: A Deacon, an ordained Priest who married and his Bishop banned him from exercising his priestly ministry, and a woman who has a hospital ministry are in the room with a dying person whose family asks to have their loved one anointed. All three, the woman, Deacon, and banned married Priest have the gift of the Holy Spirit for healing, according to Jesus, but the power corrupted Roman Hierarchy forbids them from anointing the person with the Sacrament of the sick.

How sick is this? How incredibly insensitive is this practice to the dying person and family who are desperate to experience the comforting, healing, and hope filled presence of the Holy Spirit. Is this an abuse of power or what? I think so, but don't bet on them admitting it. At best you will get a lecture on it's only the Priest who can anoint according to the epistle of

James that states if there are any sick among you, bring in the Priest and elders and anoint them with oil.

Was the Priest the only one with the gift to anoint and heal? Who were these Elders? Why do they need to go if only the Priest has the gift and authority to anoint and heal? The Priest joined the elders who you can bet on also had the gift to heal given to them by the Holy Spirit and were appointed and confirmed by the experience of the community. When the leper asked Jesus if he would heal him on the Sabbath, did Jesus say he had to get permission from the Pharisees first? He did not.

What is the difference of a Roman Catholic Priest anointing and praying for healing and other Christian denominations when their lay ministers of healing pray over and anoint people? Is there some unique magical healing that takes place because a 'Roman' Catholic Priest does it?

What the heck do people do when the nearest priest might be hundreds of miles away, like in third world countries or where there is a shortage? Like I said earlier and more critical and serious than the shortage of Priests, is the shortage of ministry and the sacraments.

A short reminder, that it is the responsibility of the Pope and Bishops to provide the sacraments for Catholics. They continue to not provide Priests to perform the sacraments. Why, because they will not consider the Spirit led Pauline communities, with the faithful having the gifts of the Holy Spirit and not just residing in one man, the Priest.

By now, you are probably getting sick of hearing the same thing over and over again, that the 'Roman' Catholic Church has put the dissemination of the Holy Spirit in the sacraments in one man, the Priest. It is intentional, why, to finally point out and call out the root and source of the evil that has and continues to destroy Catholicism. You cannot cast out the enemy if you can't identify it. May the Lord be merciful to the hierarchy, and I really mean and pray that, but also discipline and hold the guilty accountable.

**RP**: **ONLY A PRIEST CAN PREACH AND PROCLAIM THE GOSPEL** at Mass because the Priest has been given that power and authority by the 'Roman' Church. This is a bunch of baloney and another way to enhance the position of the Priest, instead of Jesus proclamation that the gift of the Holy Spirit to preach and witness is given to **ALL**. It's called **Evangelization!**

**CS: How many Priests do you know who can't preach?**

Preaching is **witnessing** to one's personal experience of the Holy Spirit and the teachings of Jesus in their daily lives, not just teaching theology from the pulpit and what the 'Church' says. They equate Teaching and Preaching as one and the same. They are not. My guess is they have not experienced the baptism of the Holy Spirit like Cornelius, the Roman centurion, nor have they been given the gift of the Holy Spirit to Preach.

Over the years, having worked with teens to seniors, there are thousands upon thousands of people sitting in the pews that have powerful stories witnessing to their experience of Jesus, the Eucharist, and the Holy Spirit, that you can see and feel the

Spirit with and in them. These are the real preachers of the Lord, but have no place in the liturgies or sacraments.

Again, the hierarchy and Priests wonder why people are leaving the 'Roman' Catholic Church. The answer is simple, they are not leaving Catholicism, but the hierarchy and the power structure of the 'Roman' church to join evangelical communities where their spiritual gifts and ministries are not only welcomed but are encouraged and given a place to use them.

Believers, touched and gifted by the Holy Spirit, are not ignorant and refuse to be a part of a 'Roman' Catholic Cult led by cult leaders and a system that stifles the Spirit from bearing fruit.

### **RC: MASS**:

- Only a Priest can say the prayers of the Canon.
- Only a Priest and ordained Deacon can Read the Gospel.
- Only a Priest or ordained Deacon can preach.
- Only the Priest or Deacon can purify and put the Ciborium back in the tabernacle.
- Only the Pastor decides to have Eucharistic ministers or not.
- Only the Priest Pastor decides whether to allow women in the sanctuary or girl altar servers.

- Only the Priest can bless children or adults who have not received their first communion. Eucharistic ministers are forbidden to bless because that power resides only in the Priest.

Those who do not agree and speak out are frightened of being reprimanded and told they are disobedient and even labeled as not being a good Catholic.

**CS**: Jesus said,

> "You make man's laws equal to God's commandments."
> (Mk. 7:8)

Does the Hierarchy really believe that people go to Mass to see and listen to the priest perform? Do they really believe that children and believers who have not made their first communion come forward for a blessing by the Priest? Did it ever dawn on them that people come forward to receive the blessing and presence of the Risen Christ in the Eucharist, whether given by the Eucharistic minister, Priest, or layperson?

I have heard from several people who work in parishes that their Priests, especially the newly ordained, constantly remind them that they are the 'Alter Christus'.

You can't make this stuff up. Where do they get this crap? I'll tell you, Seminaries and their Clerical theologians and teachers of the 'Roman' Catholic Church. For those who don't understand Latin, the title 'Alter Christus' means **another Christ.**

I thought Jesus warned us to be aware of false prophets and messiahs proclaiming themselves to be the Christ.

For all priests who believe this and use this title to demand respect and obedience, you are not an 'Alter Christus'. Catholicism and the world do **not** need another Christ. **There is only one, and you are not him**. Maybe you should get a job at Motor Vehicle verifying 'Titles'.

This is not what the Holy Spirit taught at Vatican II, that the Church is not the Hierarchy, but the 'People of God, believers baptized with and having the gifts of the Holy Spirit. These gifts were poured out to **all** believers, but many Bishops rejected the validity of Vatican II and didn't recognize the Church as 'the people of God' but little by little, over the past sixty years, have reversed Vatican II, reaffirmed and solidified the all-male power and authority of the clergy.

They have reclaimed their position and power as the sole possessors of all the gifts of the Holy Spirit. This is why the 'Roman Catholic' church since Vatican II is looking more and more like the church before the Vatican Council. *(Dominated by the Clergy)*

**Sounds like a Cult to me**. The real scandal that the all-male Hierarchy will have to face is its responsibility for the division, disillusionment, and lack of ministry for the faithful. They have starved the faithful from experiencing the Lord's healing, teaching, comfort and hope by once again claiming they are the only source of the Holy Spirit. They have become rich elite Cult leaders while the faithful have become their victims instead of their brothers and sisters.

**RC:** The Roman Catholic Church hierarchy, the Pope gathered with Bishops, are the only men who have the gift of discerning the Holy Spirit and making all the rules. Bishops, Priests and Pastors have the power and sole authority to discern the Holy Spirit for their Parishioners and make policies and rules regarding the implementation of the Spirit's directives.

**CS:** Here we go again. Discernment of the Holy Spirit has been given solely to the Pope, Bishops, and Priests. Are you starting to see a pattern here of what I mean by the 'Roman Catholic Cult' and their corrupt system of power? If you are, you are not alone, many in the past and more and more in the present are experiencing the same.

Discernment of the Holy Spirit is central to the confusion among believers. Who has the gift of discernment and how do we know what's from man and us personally, and what's truly from the Holy Spirit?

Common sense tells me that many things over the history of the 'Roman' Catholic Church were not from the Holy Spirit but by men, i.e. members of the clergy.

- Inquisitions, Crusades, Indulgences, Simony, Celibacy, ex-communications, silencing any and all dissidents, schisms and the like, are all examples that they not only got it wrong, but caused horrific suffering and death.

- The most you can expect for an answer to all these 'so called discerned' practices, policies, and teachings that proved not to be from the Holy Spirit, is 'Whoops'. Why, because they have no defense or answer.

What does discernment of the Spirit mean and how specifically does the Holy Spirit reveal itself and to whom?

These are probably the most important questions for the hierarchy and the future of the Catholic Church if it is to be a people created by the Lord and the experience of the Holy Spirit, not a program, not a pronouncement by the Roman Church or clergy. This is the truth, because God said so.

- *"Unless the Lord builds the city, the laborers labor in vain."*
 *(Ps. 121:1)*

The point here is the importance of discerning what and how the Lord reveals his will.

It has been taught that Jesus chose Peter to be the first Pope and the rock upon Jesus will build his church, possessing the authority that whatever he binds and loose here on earth will be bound in heaven.

Has anyone asked why Peter and none of the other Apostles? Read what precedes Peter's proclamation:

*[13] When Jesus came to the region of Caesarea Philippi, he asked his disciples, "Who do people say the Son of Man is?"*

*[14] They replied, "Some say John the Baptist; others say Elijah; and still others, Jeremiah or one of the prophets."*

*[15] "But what about you?" he asked. "Who do you say I am?"*

*[16] Simon Peter answered, "You are the Messiah, the Son of the living God."*

*¹⁷ Jesus replied, "Blessed are you, Simon son of Jonah, for this was not revealed to you by flesh and blood, but by my Father in heaven. ¹⁸ And I tell you that you are Peter and on this rock I will build my church, and the gates of Hades will not overcome it. ¹⁹ I will give you the keys of the kingdom of heaven; whatever you bind on earth will be bound in heaven, and whatever you loose on earth will be loosed in heaven." ²⁰ Then he ordered his disciples not to tell anyone that he was the Messiah.* (Mt. 16:13-20)

Jesus recognized that his Father gave **Peter's mind the <u>gift</u> and <u>power</u> to receive a Divine communication and Wisdom to know and experience who Jesus was**. Peter, having received this revelation, chose to believe it was a **<u>direct revelation</u>** from God by experiencing the power of its truth, and proclaimed it.

Peter, according to Jesus was given the gift of discernment by the Father, not the power and authority that everything he says is from the Holy Spirit and to be obeyed. In other words many members of the hierarchy believe that their personal beliefs, interpretations, deductions and pronouncements are from the Holy Spirit and to be accepted and obeyed without dissent or question. This RC clergy belief is BS.

Why is it BS, because of the Hierarchy's history of decisions and doctrines that were not from the Holy Spirit, instead proved to be divisive, untrue, and a disaster? How did this happen if they were the successors of Peter and the Apostles that Jesus gave the gift of discernment and the authority to proclaim it?

**The answer is that Jesus and the Father didn't give all of them this gift of discernment automatically because of their**

**appointed position and office.** What if Jesus gave Peter the keys of the Kingdom, not because of any personal skills, intelligence or attributes, but simply recognized that Peter had been given by the Father, the gift of knowing and experiencing a direct revelation and communication from God.

What if this is the criteria for all who are Bishops and Priests. Have they all been given this gift of **direct revelations from God**? I think not. Instead, they continue to believe that what they think and decide to do is **automatically** what the Holy Spirit wants because they have the Office and Position given them by others who have the office and position. This belief and mentality is so far from the gift the Father gave to Peter of direct communication with him.

This is why many Bishops and Priests have let evil and power deceive them, thinking that their personal thoughts, interpretations, and spirituality are automatically God's, without any direct revelation from him. This they claim is how the Holy Spirit works. **I DON'T THINK SO!**

## PETER'S GIFT OF DISCERNMENT GIVEN BY GOD THE FATHER AND HOW HE MANIFESTED IT

### The Council at Jerusalem *(Acts 15:1-11)*

*"Certain people came down from Judea to Antioch and were teaching the believers:* ***"Unless you are circumcised, according to the custom taught by Moses, you cannot be saved."*** *[2] This brought Paul and Barnabas into sharp dispute and debate with them.*

*So Paul and Barnabas were appointed, along with some other believers, to go up to Jerusalem to see the apostles and elders about this question. ³ The church sent them on their way, and as they traveled through Phoenicia and Samaria, they told how the Gentiles had been converted. This news made all the believers very glad.* ⁴

*When they came to Jerusalem, they were welcomed by the church and the apostles and elders, to whom they reported everything God had done through them.*

*⁵ Then some of the believers who belonged to the party of the Pharisees stood up and said,* **"The Gentiles must be circumcised and required to keep the Law of Moses."**

*⁶ The apostles and elders met to consider this question. ⁷ After much discussion,* **Peter got up and addressed them**: *"Brothers, you know that some time ago God made a choice among you that the Gentiles might hear from my lips the message of the gospel and believe.*

*⁸* **God, who knows the heart, showed that he accepted them by giving the Holy Spirit to them, just as he did to us. ⁹ He did not discriminate between us and them, for he purified their hearts by faith.** *¹⁰ Now then, why do you try to test God by putting on the necks of Gentiles a yoke that neither we nor our ancestors have been able to bear? ¹¹ No! We believe it is through the grace of our Lord Jesus that we are saved, just as they are."*

**POINT:** While others resisted and disputed Paul and Barnabas' stories and claims that the Gentiles experienced the Holy Spirit, just as the believers and Apostles did at Pentecost, Peter, because of the Gift God the Father gave him, recognized and felt the Holy Spirit in Paul and Barnabas, but also in their stories.

The others didn't understand, Peter did, **not** because he was appointed to the position of the first Pope, **not** because he was the sharpest tool in the shed, and **not** because it was his personal opinion or decision. **It was because of this 'gift' of God the Father that the Lord spoke directly to Peter and he recognized it.**

**GET IT? This gift is what is missing** in many of the clergy in the 'Roman' Catholic Church who have the offices and positions, but not the gifts from the Father and Holy Spirit.

## HOW DO WE KNOW WHAT IS OF THE HOLY SPIRIT AND WHAT IS NOT?

This question was asked of Jesus. He answered it in the parable of the fig tree that didn't bear fruit. He said if it doesn't bear fruit, cut it down and throw it into the fire. In other words, if it doesn't help people to experience the unconditional love of the God and the Holy Spirit, if it doesn't lead them into a personal daily dialogue relationship with Jesus, and if it doesn't help believers to discern the Lord's Will for them, then stop listening to those who claim that Jesus and the Father have given them the authority and power of discernment but did not.

**POINT:** According to Jesus how to determine what is from the Spirit and what is from man is 'bearing fruit'. If the laws, teachings, and sacraments are **not** bearing fruit, then stop doing it that way, as stated before.

This is simple and common sense, but many in power are in denial and will not give up their power and system of control to ordinary people who God himself chooses to give the gift to know his thoughts and Will. He also gives them the knowledge to distinguish them from their own personal ideas, interpretations and spirituality, and have them verified and confirmed by others who have the gift.

One of my questions to the clergy is, do you believe in the gift of Prophecy? Another is, do you understand how the gift works? Lastly, do you have this necessary gift of the Holy Spirit to know God's Will, and lead? If they don't, then don't panic, but read and ask the Lord for the gift of Prophecy that will catapult you from your position of authority and business to 'walking with Jesus every day, all day.

Listen to how the gift of Prophecy and discernment works within communities of faith.

## PROPHECY- DISCERNMENT, AND THE CHURCH

*By Ralph F. Wilson,* The Holy Spirit as the Agent of Renewal, *unpublished doctoral dissertation, Fuller Theological Seminary, 1984, pp. 149-154*

*The great value of prophecy to the church today is the contemporary Word of God to encourage and guide his people.[13] The prophetic message is "a word fitly spoken"*

*(Proverbs 25:11),* **Directly From God,** *"good for edifying, as fits the occasion, that it may impart grace to those who hear" (Ephesians 4:29).*

*A specific revelation can be particularly powerful in bringing conviction of sin and of God's presence to unbelievers or backsliders who are present in a church gathering. Paul suggests to the Corinthians how prophecy can work in this way:*

1. *If **all** prophesy, and an unbeliever or outsider enters, he is convicted by all, he is called to account by all, the secrets of his heart are disclosed; and so, falling on his face, he will worship God and declare that God is really among you (1 Corinthians 14:24-25). For the outsider,* **prophecy can be a powerful sign of God's presence among His people.**

2. *Problems with individuals in the body or with the body itself may also be pinpointed by the gift of prophecy. James Dunn observes.*

3. **"Prophecy prevents a man pretending to be other than he is--prevents the believer hiding behind a mask of pretended righteousness, of apparent spirituality.** *At any time the prophetic word may expose him for what he is."[14]*

4. *Thus prophecy builds up the church by converting the unbeliever and purifying the believer.*

5. *The variety of ways the church is built up by prophecy accentuates its necessity for the present day church.*

6. *Words of comfort and assurance, words of pleading,* **words of exhortation and admonition, words of exposure and correction--all of these are designed by the Spirit to bring and maintain renewal in Christ's church.**

**We cannot afford to despise the gift of prophecy**, *nor can we allow its capacity for misuse and misunderstanding prevents us from embracing it. Rather we must diligently seek to curb its abuses by the guidelines of Scripture and* **"Test all things"** *(1 Thessalonians 5:20-21), so that the great constructive value of prophecy may be experienced by our churches.[15] Through this unique spiritual gift the church is enabled to grow, mature and move forward according to the will of God.*

*"Make love your aim, and earnestly desire the spiritual gifts, <u>especially that you may prophesy</u> ... so that the church may be edified"* (1 Cor. 14:1, 5).

**SUMMARY:** Discernment of the Holy Spirit and Prophesy are those, like Peter, who have been given the gift to have God directly reveal his Will and word to them for the community and the church in general. To validate it, it needs to be confirmed by others who have the gift. Not just the hierarchy, but all of us may have a bit of the Truth.

In terms of the present state of the 'Roman' Catholic Church and its Roman system of the sole authority and dissemination of the Holy Spirit and Sacraments, residing only in the clergy, is no longer bearing fruit and the Lord is saying,

*"Stop doing it this way... Stop trying to put the 'New wine in the old wine skin."*

Why, because when you only try to change words, tweak liturgies, to reestablish the old ways, theologies that are not bearing fruit, **you are insane**.

*"Doing the same thing over and over again expecting different results is the definition of insanity."*

# CHAPTER 9

# WHAT ARE SOME OF THE DIFFERENT WAYS THE LORD COMMUNICATES WITH US

I've always believed that it's OK to criticize and point out others weaknesses and faults, but you better have answers and solutions that help the person change and be set free.

An important note and reminder, that I have no intention of attacking or judging any one specifically in the clergy from the Pope on down, but like St. Francis offer how the Holy Spirit can and will reform the corrupt 'Roman' system and deliver evil from our Catholic faith.

As I have pointed out how power has corrupted the 'Roman' church clerical leadership over the centuries, Jesus has pointed us to the discernment of the Holy Spirit as the answer.

How then does the Holy Spirit communicate the Lord's Will to us personally? How does the Holy Spirit reveal the Lord's Will to Bishops and Priests in positions of authority?

If they don't know how, then they settle for

- A democratic vote, the majority wins.

- Who has the best idea?

- What is the most practical and efficient way.

- Who has the most influence and the Pastor's or Bishop's ear?

- What has worked in the past, just keep the status quo.

- The personal preferences and ideas of the Priest or Bishop.

- Choosing the path of least resistance.

## **YOUR DAILY ADVENTURE WITH JESUS**

Even if you have been baptized by the Holy Spirit, what you are about to learn from Jesus may offer new gifts and new doors to open and follow for the clergy.

When you have been baptized with the Holy Spirit and have passed over into the Kingdom of God, then your adventure with Jesus begins.

Remember how and when you experience the Holy Spirit is between you and the Lord, according to when he thinks you are ready. Your adventure with the Lord is unique and different from everyone else's, because you are unique. Yet a relationship is a relationship and requires communication. For a personal relationship to deepen and grow, it must be a **dialogue** and not a **monologue**, talking **and listening**.

When people ask me how to deepen their faith and relationship with Jesus, I first ask them how they pray. Then I ask them what percentage of it is a monologue and what percentage is a dialogue. After that I say "to deepen your faith and relationship with Jesus, you need to learn how to listen to him and how he communicates with you. In other words, Jesus actually reveals himself to you with wisdom, direction and God's Will for you each day, whatever you are doing and wherever you are.

Now I want to ask you, the clergy and whoever is reading this, what is the percentage of your communication with God that is a dialogue? Is it mostly a monologue with you doing all the talking? The question here that Jesus wants to answer is that **YES**, he can and does want you to trust him with everything and anything that you want or need. But more importantly, he wants you to **listen to him** and know that he is with you and will be forever.

**THIS IS THE ADVENTURE**: to grow in awareness, not only believing that Jesus is with you, but experiencing and TRUSTING that he really is and revealing his Will every day all day.

## THE WAY TO KNOW HIS WILL IS TRUST

*"In God we trust"* we've heard over and over again, but nobody taught us how to specifically and actually do it.

Jesus did, but have the clergy taught us how? I hope and pray they have.

Let Jesus explain and show us how to. Every Christian, especially those in the Hierarchy and positions of authority should learn, memorize, and do it according to Jesus way. We need to know the difference between **Faith** and **Trust**.
**Faith is what** you believe. It is in the mind, thoughts, truths, theology, and beliefs. *(Example: The Apostles' Creed)* Faith is our great gift from God, but to know God, and I mean really know him and his love, is not with information, theology, commandments, or stories about him.

It is through **TRUST** that we know him, by experiencing and becoming intimately one with him. Think about it this way. A wife knows and could list all the positive qualities and information about her husband. Are all these qualities the **LOVE** she feels toward him? I don't think so, and I bet neither does she. If I found another man, who has even better qualities than her husband, would she still love him? The answer is that the love she has for her husband is not the sum total of his positive qualities, rather her experience of his love and affection for her.

**TRUST** is an action verb and a choice made with your Will. It is not information, thoughts or feelings in your mind. It is that choice to trust, let go, and be vulnerable that opens the door to our heart and soul, to experience and feel another's presence *(Their consciousness, mind, and soul)*. By just having faith and believing in Jesus, we operate only with our thoughts, feelings and minds and express our love for the Lord by reciting prayers, devotions and rituals. Peace, Joy, Life, Forgiveness, Healing, Hope, Strength, and love come through **Trusting** in Jesus.

Now, if Trust is how we know the Lord and the Holy Spirit, then how do we do it? The answer is in the following parable. Can you figure it out?

## PARABLE OF THE HIGH WIRE WALKER

There was a high wire walker that millions of people would come from all over the world, just to get a glimpse of him perform incredible and impossible things on the wire without a net, 100 feet in the air.

For one hour he did things that were spell bounding and just down right impossible.

At the end of the hour, there was a grand silence, and the spectators were in awe from what they had seen. He came down from the wire, approached somebody in the bleachers, and said to them, "What do you think?" The person responded, "I think that I have never seen anything like what I just witnessed."

The high wire walker then looked the person in the eye and asked, "Who do you say that I am?" The person paused and then said, "From what I've seen, I think that you are the greatest high wire walker that has and will ever live."

"Good," said the high wire walker and looked at the person in the eye again. "Do you believe in me?" The person said, "Yes, I do believe in you." Then the high wire walker said, "Do you see this wheelbarrow here? It has a smooth solid glass wheel in the front. There are no treads or grooves on it. I am going to bring it up 100 ft. and walk it across the wire, but I am going to chain my hands to the handles, so if the wheelbarrow slips off the wire, and it falls a 100 feet to the ground, I will fall with it."

With great love for the person, the high wire walker looked deep into the person's eyes again and said, "Do you believe I can do that?" The person responded with confidence: "YES, I do believe you can do that!"

Then, with the greatest compassion, the high wire walker said to the person,

**"Good…now get in the wheelbarrow! ….. I beg you … get in the wheelbarrow"**

If we do not trust *(Get in the wheelbarrow)*, we are left alone with only our problems, suffering, fear, worry, doubt and despair *(On the bleachers).* This is why many people become angry with God, leave church, and even lose faith. They believe in God and Jesus, but only if he answers all their prayers and fixes their problems, because if God really loves them, he should heal them and make their problems go away immediately. This kind of thinking is Evil's way of keeping believers from having a trusting relationship with Jesus. *(Getting in the wheel barrow)*

If we do have a personal relationship with Jesus, Evil will have less and less influence and power over us, why, because we are in the wheelbarrow with Jesus, conquering fear together. My guess is that St. Paul and the early Christians were persecuted and executed because of their faith, but experienced the power and love of Christ that was greater than their fear of suffering and death. They trusted and got in the wheelbarrow.

- *"The power in us now is greater than the powers that are in the world." (1 Jn. 4:4)*

- *"The sufferings of the present are as nothing compared to the glory that God will manifest in us." (Rom. 8:18)*

## STEPS TO TRUST: WHAT TO DO

No matter what thoughts are in your mind, and no matter how intense your feelings and emotions are:

1. Choose (with your Will) to focus off of the problem, fear, or whatever is tempting you.

2. Focus on Jesus with you by simply saying, "Lord."

3. Choose to stay focused on Jesus and say **NO** to your thoughts, feelings and emotions.

4. Rest in His presence until you find Peace of Mind, whether you experience him, or not.

5. Lastly, replace your negative thoughts, half-truths, and lies that are in your mind causing your fears, worries, and stress— with the Truth and presence of the Lord.

6. Then do His Will no matter what you think or feel, constantly aware that he is with you, giving you strength and power to overcome anything.

You really need to imprint the above steps into your mind, memorize them, and from now on call them to mind throughout your day. When you have problems, suffer or have decisions to make, build a **TRUST** relationship with the Lord. The heart of this book is that Jesus is teaching us how to experience the Lord as the Truth, the Life, and the Way, to answer our questions about our journey with him as Catholics, what to do and how to do it.

## **WHAT THE ROMAN CLERGY AND MANY OF US FORGOT WHEN WE GREW UP IS, HOW TO TRUST**

I want you to use your memory and imagination.

- Remember when you were four and not yet in school. See yourself back then.

- Remember how you clung to your mother.

- Remember when your mother told you that you could play outside, but stay in the yard. See yourself playing in the yard.

- **OUCH!** Remember falling and cutting your knee on the sidewalk and seeing it bleed? You were frightened and screamed, and it sure did hurt. Can you see it?

- What was the first word out of your mouth? That's right: **"Mommy!"**

You had only one thing in your mind, and it was not a thing, it was Mommy. Then you ran as fast as you could to Mommy. See yourself doing that. The minute Mommy saw you crying and your knee bleeding, she picked you up and held you. Your arms were wide open for her embrace. Then your mother held you until you finally calmed down and stopped crying.

- Now, what did you feel from your Mommy that made you stop crying?

- Be specific now and list what you experienced and felt when your mother embraced you. .

- My guess is that you felt comfort, safety, and love.

**QUESTIONS FOR YOU:**
- Were you still afraid? My guess is you were not after experiencing your mother's love.

- Did your knee still hurt? Yes.

Well, what do you know? Let's get this straight, your knee was still bleeding and hurting, but you were OK. You were OK because you did not just believe in your mother's love, but trusted her *(Got in the wheelbarrow)* and experienced it, how, by focusing immediately off the problem and instead on Mommy.

Where was the love, comfort and safety you felt? It was in your mother, because it was your mother, and when she embraced and held you, it passed from her into you, and delivered you from your fear. Did your problem (boo-boo) go away immediately? No, but you were OK.

**CONCLUSION:**
At four years old, you automatically and instinctively followed all the steps to TRUST perfectly.
**Hmm, now that's interesting, isn't it?**

Everything we needed to learn in this life, we knew when we were four, **Trust**. What happened to you and me that has put us back into Kindergarten, worried and frightened about all of our problems, suffering, decisions and boo-boos in life? We grew up— that is what happened, and because we did, we lost and forgot how to Trust, especially in the Lord.

We became our own God, and little by little no longer reached out for the Lord's wisdom, comfort, strength and healing. Why do we need to focus immediately on Jesus first when we cut our knee or have a problem? We can just call 911, a doctor, or get a Band-Aid. We can get a job, make money, and buy what we want.

"Who needs God? I can do it by myself. I am in control of my life." In short, we have become more and more independent. This is very important, because now you are beginning to understand why sometimes it feels like the Lord doesn't care, help, or answer your prayers.

## **WHAT MIGHT JESUS SAY ABOUT TRUST AS THE ANSWER FOR OUR CHURCH LEADERSHIP TO EXPERIENCE AND KNOW THE LORD'S WILL**

### **JESUS:**
*"Now you know why I said, "Unless you become like little children, you will never enter the Kingdom of God." Because of Evil, you have been seduced into believing that you have total control of your life. It is a false sense of control that distracts and draws your attention away from me and focuses your attention on the pleasure of power and control. The reason it is false is because the physical, mental, and emotional suffering you experience is out of control.*

*This is where all your fear, worrying, discouragement and despair come from. Then, you pray and ask me to fix it so you can find Peace of mind and rest, and when it does not go away, you blame me for not caring or loving you. This is what Evil wants you to do, not believe or trust me. At that moment, when you choose not to trust me, you are alone with your problems and suffering, without hope. This is exactly where Evil has led you, to despair.*

*That is what I meant when I said "You must become like little children." You need to retrain your mind, like when you were four years old, and do exactly what you said and did back then. Instead of "Mommy", say "Lord" and then focus off your problem, pain, suffering, and focus on me with your whole mind, with no other thought or desire than to experience my embrace. Then you will find your answer and what's more, that I, your Lord, love you. So, remember this truth. I did not come into the world to fix everybody, everything, and all of your problems.*

*I came into the world to conquer your fear of them, give you rest, and then overcome them together with the power that I overcame mine. So keep paying attention and burning the way to trust into your mind, until it replaces the way Evil and the world has taught you. Most of all, remember, I love you and believe in you. Amen!"*

**JESUS NEVER SAID:** *"Come to me all you who labor and are heavy burdened and **I will fix everything.**"*

**JESUS SAID:** *"Come to me all you who labor and are heavy burdened and **I will give you Rest.**"* (Mt. 11:28)

Just like what our mothers/parents did, Jesus is waiting 24/7 to calm us down, give us rest, peace of mind, and deliver us from our fear. This is good news from the Lord himself for Bishops, Priests, and the Roman Hierarchy as what gift to ask for from the Holy Spirit, to discern God's Will and be unafraid to do it.

## **THE DIFFERENT WAYS THE LORD COMMUNICATES WITH US PERSONALLY**

These are the gifts of the Holy Spirit that the Clergy and Hierarchy must seek and be given in order to discern and lead.

**THROUGH A SITUATION:**
A young man named Tim, senior in college, decided to take an alternative spring break and volunteered for a week at St. Francis Inn Soup Kitchen in Philadelphia. His plan was to get his master's degree in engineering, but after living and working with the poor, feeding them, waiting on and befriending them, he experienced the Holy Spirit and Jesus. In his own words, "I actually felt Jesus in the people when I spent time talking to and serving them."

Does the Lord communicate and reveal his Will to us? You bet he does. How do I know that? Tim postponed his grad school plans and volunteered two more years at the soup kitchen.

**THROUGH THE WORD OF GOD:** When my sister faced cancer and surgery, she was overcome by fear and worry. She initially asked the Lord for a miracle. When her fear intensified and she became more anxious, she opened her Bible and read words of

Jesus that jumped off the page, as if Jesus was right there saying them to her personally, "While you are in the world you will suffer, but don't be afraid, for I am with you. Trust in God and trust in me."

She prayed for healing, but prayed for the grace to trust in Jesus and let go of her fear by not dwelling on her cancer and surgery. Instead she focused on the Lord with her and on doing things she would ordinarily do to keep her attention from centering on her cancer. It was not magic, because that's not how Trust works.

She was still tempted and attacked by fear, but kept choosing to tell Jesus she trusted Him, and she let go. Little by little, the grace she asked for was given to her, because she experienced peace and less and less fear and worry.

The day of her surgery, two of her friends and I were waiting for the doctors to call her down. We prayed with her and again she simply said, "I trust in you, Jesus. Your Will be done." When we finished, my sister who has a great wit, made us laugh with funny one-liners about her surgery. All of us, my sister included, felt absolutely no fear or worry.

When the doctor and nurse walked in, we were having a full belly laugh. Later the doctor told my sister that in all his years doing surgery, he never experienced someone so unafraid and overcome with laughter as they wheeled her into surgery. My sister told him that Jesus told her to trust Him, and she did. Does Jesus communicate and reveal his Will for us through his words? You bet He does. Just ask my sister.

**DIRECT FROM THE LORD**:
My brother, a diocesan priest for 53 years who recently graduated to eternal life, while on a long retreat as a young priest, received two direct words from the Lord, calling him to a prophetic preaching ministry. He made the leap of faith and trusted in the Lord, and his life and ministry changed radically.

Since that time he has preached and given the Lord's Word and prophecies to many thousands of people all over the United States and Europe. He has also prophesied to the institutional church, parishes, and individuals. Like many prophets, he was mocked, belittled, and considered a 'persona non grata'.

However, by trusting in the Lord and living by the guidance of the Holy Spirit, Jesus has been able to forgive, heal, guide, and give hope to more people than he would have if my brother stayed in parish ministry. Does Jesus reveal His Will and plan for our lives directly? He did to my brother!

> *"For to one is given by the Spirit the Word of Wisdom, to another the Word of Knowledge by the same Spirit." (1 Cor. 12:8)*

**CHURCH TEACHINGS:** All Christian religions believe in the forgiveness of our sins, because of Jesus shedding His blood on the cross with the saving words, "Father, forgive them for they know not what they do."

Phil is a man I visited in a maximum-security prison who had attempted suicide a couple times for his horrific crimes, feeling nothing left to live for. He was an atheist his whole life and lived according to his own desires and beliefs. I told him there was another way besides suicide, and that I knew how to lead him there, without preaching to him or trying to proselytize him.

In short, I told him that the God who created him would not only forgive him, but he unconditionally loved him before he sinned, while he was sinning, and after he sinned.

I left him with a decision to make. If you hate your life, would you be willing to give it to Jesus and ask for his forgiveness? He said "yes" the following week, and we prayed together. When he was praying and surrendering his life to Jesus, he burst into hysterical sobbing, and all of his guilt and self- hatred poured out. Then he looked up at me, half-dazed and said, "Jesus is really here, isn't he?" I said, "I guess so, and he really loves you."

The Christian church teaches that Jesus forgives our sins. Ask Phil if he not only believes this, but experienced it. Phil is no longer an atheist.

**THROUGH OTHERS:** *(Sometimes the most unlikely)* Yes, the Lord can and does answer our prayers through other people, and sometimes by those we least expect. They can even be unaware that they are the answer to your prayer. The Lord can bring more out of this way of answering your prayers, because you just may be the answer to theirs. The Lord doesn't force us, but sets up the connection of people and hopes we are open to giving to one another not only answers but also Peace of Mind, healing, and even forgiveness. Let me explain.

**PERSONAL STORY**: When I was at a soup kitchen in Philadelphia where we fed 300+ people a day, twice a day, we friars lived across the street from the kitchen in a row house in what the TV program Nightline, at that time, reported was one of worst neighborhoods in the United States.

There were always five to ten people sleeping on cardboard on the sidewalk in front of our door and at the soup kitchen. I couldn't sleep one night, decided to go across the street to the soup kitchen to get some milk.

For two or three weeks, I was going through the motions, but inside I was "burnt out," getting conned, threatened, and constantly ripped off. I started becoming cynical and questioned what I was doing with my life. I sure did not feel like a Franciscan priest or 'brother' to the people. When I walked out of the friary onto a piece of cardboard, there he was, "Cincinnati", as he wanted to be called. He was one of the worst con men at the kitchen, and I was his worst confronter. We were like oil and water.

So he immediately woke up as I opened the door, got up on his knees and told me he had to go to the bathroom and that he was hungry. I wasn't in the mood for his lies and con job, so my first response was "No". Then he kept demanding and begging as usual. So, reluctantly, he followed me to the soup kitchen. I opened the door of the bathroom and waited for him to finish. As he left, he saw two donuts left over from the day before and asked to take them, once again in his demanding voice. I simply said take them. All I wanted to do was get a glass of milk.

When I finished and started walking back to the friary, I remember thinking "Not a great start of the day again, Lord. I have no idea where you are and what's happening to me."

When I got to the friary door, there was Cincinnati waiting for me. What did he want now? Then he put his hand on my shoulder, looked at me with a look that I had never seen before, touched my cheek, and with a heartfelt voice said, "Brother Francis, you are a real Brother."

After three weeks of self-pity, the Lord spoke and reminded me who and what I was, that he had been with me and loved me. That's the adventure of the Lord. His answer to my prayer came through a poor homeless person named Cincinnati.

After that morning, we became friends, but he still conned me. However, it was a lot less. And when he did, we'd both laugh. So keep your spiritual eyes and ears open for the answers to your prayers, because Jesus is full of surprises. You can end up with more than you ask for.

**CONNECTING DOTS: GUARANTEED 'ADVENTURE'**
Did you ever meet someone, a complete stranger, and circumstances led you to help them? Or, they helped you in a way that really answered both of your prayers? Afterwards, as you reflected on it, you felt that it was not a coincidence, rather it had been planned by the Lord without forcing you to recognize, help, or even heal one another.

When I said that discerning the Lord's Will is the great adventure the he offers us every day by discovering his plan for us, and not just ours for him—I call it **'Connecting the Dots'**.

Do you remember that coloring book where we didn't see the whole picture until we looked for and found the next dot to connect them all? For me, this has been and continues to be the most exciting way to discover and do God's Will.
This is how it works for me. I have my list of things I want or have to do each day, but I am open and look for God's dots that start connecting.

Then the more I connect them, the more I know it's not a coincidence, but him revealing his Will to me for the person or the situation I'm in. The moment I **'get it'** and see the whole picture, I can sense the Lord with me, offering his answer to a prayer. Many times, he answers mine at the same time through a person or the situation I'm in. When it's over, there is the realization that this was a God moment and experience, because we connected the dots.

**STORYTIME:** The windshield on my car was hit by a stone and cracked. Besides being another thing I had to do, the only time they could get me in to fix it was a day that I was booked and busy. Pain in the neck I thought.

So, I started the day frustrated and overwhelmed because of having to rush across town get the darn windshield fixed so I could get on with what I had to do. After I checked in I was told that it would take an hour and a half. Great news! So, there I sat in the waiting room mumbling to myself and to the Lord, "Why me?" Sound familiar?

The minute I sat down, a young woman came in to have her windshield fixed. When she sat down, I sensed that she was troubled. After the usual hello and casual talk, I asked her if she was ok. She began to cry and told me that she had just come from the hospital where she said her mother was dying, but had come to get her windshield fixed because it was the only time they could fit her in.

We began to talk at length and I shared with her what the Lord had taught me about suffering and death, and how he is with us to help us through it. At the end I asked her if I could pray with her to experience the Lord with her and her mother. She said "Yes" and welcomed it. So we prayed, and all during the prayer she wept and let out all the fear and worrying that she held inside.

After we prayed, she gave me a hug and said "I think the Lord sent you." **Bingo!** We **'connected the dots'**. Both of us thought that the reason we had the same appointment time was to get our windows fixed. That was our plan, but the Lord's plan was that each of us was the answer to each other's prayer. I immediately realized that this was the Lord's plan all along for me. That's why my response to her saying that God had sent me was, **"He did."**

Connecting the dots is the most exciting way that the Lord reveals His will every day. I strongly suggest you ask the Lord to reveal his Will for you by giving you the gift of looking for and recognizing **'the non- coincidence dots'**.

## THE 1% WAY TO DISCERN GOD'S WILL

The Lord taught me this when I was in my early twenties as I decided that he was calling me to priesthood. I call it the 1% prayer. Up until then I asked God to help me with serious decisions by telling me what I should do and what his Will was. However, most of the time I didn't feel as if God was listening and certainly not telling me what I should do. I even said in my prayer that I was "thick and dumb" and needed his answer to be obvious and crystal clear. That didn't work either.

Then I received some great spiritual direction. A holy person told me that Jesus is always going to respect my freedom to choose, because he knows that is how we will learn to trust. Then he gave me a formula when asking for God's input in decision-making, **bingo**, the **1% discernment method**. Before this, I always expected the Lord to give me the answer with 100% certitude and make it completely obvious.

Well, here it is. I have made every major decision in life, using the 1% method, and the Lord has taught me that it works. If you have a choice to make between two paths to take, and are attached to both at 50% each, unable to make a decision, stop asking the Lord for 100% certitude. Just ask Him for 1%, be patient and wait. Keep asking and keep your spiritual ears and eyes open. But let go of it.

When you are ready, and many times when you least expect it, he will give you the 1%. The best part is that you will know that it is not from you, but him. Now, here is better news, because it's only 1%, you can still have 49% leaning toward or convinced of the other way. This is how the Lord gives you the opportunity to TRUST in him by trusting in the 1%.

This is how I had to break off the relationship with a wonderful young woman that I was pursuing and enter the seminary. I can tell you it was very difficult, but that was my choice... to trust in the Lord. It was an extremely lonely year with many doubts, but by the end of the year, I was at 55% and decided to keep trusting the now 5%. In the end, I became a deacon at about 80% and a priest at around 90%.

It's been that way for my whole priesthood, but now that I am an old friar, it's 99%. Yet 1% of me always wonders what my life would have been like if I chose the other path. And because I'm still in this life, that's OK.

So, does the Lord help us with our decisions, reveal his plan and Will to us? The author of this book says **ABSOLUTELY!**

## YOU ARE UNIQUE:
Because God created you so wonderfully unique, and the relationship you have with the Lord is between you and him, he may have given you a personalized way to reveal himself and his Will for you. All the above that I have learned from people's experience, as well as my own, you can add to yours. That should keep you busy walking with the Lord!

## KNOWING THE DIFFERENCE BETWEEN YOUR WILL AND THE LORD'S WILL GIVE YOU PEACE

The last thing I want to share with you, regarding discernment of the Lord's Will, is the importance of knowing the difference between Gods Will *(what he wants us to do)* and your **will for** him and the Church.

I invite all believers, especially those in positions of leadership ministry, whether you are the pastor, bishop, rabbi, imam, or director of a ministry in your community, to listen carefully to the following.

Jesus teaches us to discern God's Will **(What he wants us to do, and not what we think he wants.)** If you don't learn this and spend most of your time doing everything for everybody because you think this is what you are supposed to do for the Lord, the Church, and his people, you're heading for disaster.

This way of thinking is a recipe for frustration and feeling overwhelmed, not to mention the effects on your physical and mental health. You might also add your spiritual health to the mix. The answer is to ask the Holy Spirit for the Gift of Discernment, to know the difference between the two.

Since you now know the ways Jesus reveals his Will to us - learning the difference will help you to say "**No**", and that you are not available, or refer them to someone who would be able to help them, and do it without guilt. It will also help you to say '**Yes**' to those things the Lord wants you to do.

**A STORY TO REMIND YOU:**

**A gift for Mom**: People give what they want, not what the other really needs.

Three children who lived in desperate poverty with their widowed mother, left home, went out on their own, and became multi-millionaires. Getting together on their cell phones, they discussed the gifts they were able to give their elderly mother for her birthday.

- **Steve**, the oldest said, "I built a big mansion for mom. It cost two million dollars, now ma can get out of that 3 room tenant apartment."

- **Lisa** said, "Wow that's terrific. I sent Ma a Rolls Royce with all the whistles on it and a driver available 24/7. Now she can get out of that dump and go whenever and wherever she wants to."

- **Christopher**, the youngest said, "I've got you both beat. You know how mom enjoys reading the bible, and you know she can't see very well anymore? I sent her a **parrot** that can recite the entire bible. It took 20 monks in a monastery 12 years to teach the parrot. I had to pledge to contribute $100,000.00 a year for 10 years, but it was worth it. Mom just has to name the chapter and verse, and the parrot will recite it.

**Well, mom sent out her letters of Thank You cards:**
- "Steve," she wrote her eldest son, "The mansion you built is too big. I live in only one room, but I have to clean the whole house."

- "Lisa", she wrote, "I am too old to travel. I stay home all the time, so I never use the Car and the driver you hired is rude!"

- **"Christopher, my Christopher"** she wrote to her youngest son, **"you were the only one who knew what your mother really wanted."**

## THE CHICKEN WAS DELICIOUS!"     Love Mom

**POINT:** When was the last time you asked the Lord what he wanted you to do or be, and most importantly expected he could and would answer you in the different ways he reveals his Will?

This, like I said before, next to being baptized with the Holy Spirit at Pentecost, is the most important gift that is lacking in the clergy, the gift of discernment between their will for God and the church, and God's Will.

**MOTHERS**: I bet if the three children would have asked their mother what she wanted for her birthday, she would have told them to come home and spend time together with her. Sounds about right, but they didn't ask.

**HELP FOR ALL IN MINISTRY:**
Not knowing the difference between what I want to do for the church and God and knowing what he wants me to do, is a recipe for 'burnout' and 'discouragement'.

This is why a dialogue relationship with Jesus through the Holy Spirit's gift of discernment is essential.

# CHAPTER 10

# THE 'ROMAN' CATHOLIC CHURCH'S NEED FOR A NEW PENTECOST

Why, because Jesus said so, not me. He did it once at Vatican II, but the Hierarchy didn't listen and learn how to discern the Holy Spirit personally. Power and their positions of authority seduced them to do it the old way, which was 'their' way.

The mess the church is in is the result of that power grab. However, the Lord loves his church and promised the gates of hell would not prevail against it, though evil seems to be winning now.

The Lord is giving the 'Roman' Church one last chance to deliver itself from the systemic evil that has infected it. That evil has affected every aspect of the church, especially the leadership.

The answer is the Holy Spirit who will teach us ALL things and create a new wine skin to replace the old.

**The following is a rough draft for the church, the 'people of God' to discern what needs to be changed, delivered, and done for the Holy Spirit to make all things new.**

## WHO MAKES UP THIS NEW VATICAN ASSEMBLY?

- Lay people, **women and men, poor and rich, baptized with the Holy Spirit** from different Spirit-led movements and groups with delegates who have the **gifts of**

**discernment and prophecy,** experienced and appointed by their community

- Clergy who have experienced the baptism of the Holy Spirit and given the gift of discernment and Prophecy

  These are not appointed by the hierarchy, but by people who have experienced these specific gifts in the Priest, Bishop, or Deacon. **There is no need or place for Vatican Police whose power is threatened by this discernment of the Holy Spirit.**

- Evangelical ministers, brothers and sisters who have the gifts of the spirit, who have been experienced by their members and therefore recognized and appointed by their community

- **LEADERSHIP**: This Council of 'Making all things New' should be organized and led by predominately Lay people from all parts of the world, women and men, baptized with the Spirit, who have the gift of being an **'Apostoloi'** according to St. Paul's understanding of the Title.

  The Greek word **'Apostoloi'** means Messenger, True believer, Promoter, Herald, Preacher and Advocate, a person who actively supports or favors a cause, *(Not necessarily a Bishop, but people who possess the above gifts)*

## THE AGENDA

- What in the Roman Catholic Church and its past and present structure has kept believers from experiencing the Holy Spirit and the gifts of the Spirit that the Father promised to lead and minister to and with one another?

- The structure of the Clerical Hierarchy centered on Priesthood as those possessing the sole power to administer all the sacraments

- Celibacy, has it become more important than the Sacraments, especially the Eucharist?

- What in the Sacraments and the way they are administered liturgically keeps people from experiencing the unconditional love of the Risen Christ, when they receive them?

- Why, when we gather together for prayer, meetings, committees, Mass, or liturgies, people are bored, don't experience the Holy Spirit or unable to express it, so the room doesn't 'shake' with loud praises because they feel **unfed** spiritually?

- Why are the gifts of the Holy Spirit limited to only the Priests, Bishops and Deacons? Why and when in our past did that happen and why? Is it bearing 'fruit' and vocations? Why not?

- Probably the most important study and reflection of the Holy Spirit making our Catholic tradition and faith anew is the model of the Pauline communities and how the

Spirit provided, as promised, the necessary gifts for leadership and ministry, different gifts but the same Spirit. Very important is, that one is not more important than the others- "One body with many parts."

- **This is where our evangelical sisters and brothers, whose communities are Spirit centered and led by the gifts can contribute greatly, as how to ask, discern, and manifest the various gifts to lead, witness, and minister.**

- How do we transition from a 'Roman' Hierarchy structure to a Holy Spirit led Catholic Church with the Risen Christ, the **Eucharist, at its center**?

- New ways, based on scripture and the early Christians, to experience the Lord's forgiveness, healing, deliverance, his presence in the Eucharist, and the role of the Priest in the community and his necessary gifts

  **EXAMPLE**: Is the role of the priest to preside at the 'breaking of the bread', appointed locally by the community, because when he/she breaks the bread those gathered experience the Holy Spirit in them by their expressed personal love for the Lord?

  **POSSIBLE RESULTS**: There would be no shortage of Priests because there would be many in the community given the gift to preside by the Holy Spirit, recognized by their sisters and brothers. There would be no need for missionaries or Priests from other countries, who many times can't be understood, or Priests from other parishes. Each community will have their own, and more than one at that, all chosen by the communities discernment of the Holy Spirit. *(Like the first Christian communities)*

**"See, I set before you today life and death. Choose LIFE!"**

*(Deut. 30:15)*

# CHAPTER 11

## A WARNING AND INVITATION

## JESUS AND ST. PAUL'S WARNING AND INVITATION TO THE CLERGY AND HIERARCHY

- *"The Advocate, the Holy Spirit, whom my Father will send in my name, will teach you **ALL** things and remind you of everything I told you." (Jesus)*

St. Paul warned when this **gift of discernment** is not being exercised in the church, distortion of the truth occurs.

- *"See to it that no one takes you captive through hollow and deceptive philosophy, which depends on human tradition and the elemental spiritual forces of this world rather than on Christ"*

- *"The Spirit clearly says that in later times some will **abandon the faith and follow deceiving spirits and things taught by demons.**"  (I Timothy 4:1)*

As believers today, you and I are to heed that instruction to test worldly philosophies, foreign doctrines, and even new perspectives and ideas that come out of the mouths of politicians, celebrities, community leaders, and even pastors and **religious leaders.**

## SPEAKING OUT AGAINST THE CORRUPTION

Speaking out and challenging those in the hierarchy who have been seduced by power will probably result in you being chastised for disobedience to your Bishop and fear of punishment. Remember the greatest power of Evil is fear.

Be willing to accept the consequences as Jesus and St. Francis did.

When I laid prostrate in the sanctuary before I went up to the Bishop to be ordained, I was trying to focus all my thoughts and mind on Jesus, that with my whole being commit my life to him and the gift of priesthood that I believed the Holy Spirit had given to me. For me it was a promise, with the help of his grace, to obey and live according to his Will and the Gospel.

The Bishop asked me to promise obedience to the Church, to him, and his successors. I did promise to be obedient to the Church, to him, and his successors.

Over the years, I watched eight of my twelve classmates ordained that day leave active ministry in the following years, many to get married. I watched them no longer able to minister the sacraments with the gifts Jesus and the Holy Spirit gave them, because of the Church's man-made requirement of celibacy. I watched and experienced Bishops, Priests, and Pastors, using **disobedience** and **fear of reprisal** to impose their will on fellow priests and people, in the name of the 'Church'.

After many years of anger and disillusionment, I knew there was something in my soul that just didn't seem to connect with my ordination and the promises I made that day. So, I spent many years trying to reconcile obedience to the Bishop, the Church, and the Lord. Finally, one day when I was reading the scripture, it became clear to me how obedience worked, and the promises I made on ordination day.

Subsequently, for many years now I've said it to Bishops, Pastors, and others in authority.

My obedience is **FIRST** to Jesus, and his gospel; what he said, taught, and did.

**SECOND** is my obedience to the Catholic Church, the Creed, and teachings of the Church, to inform my conscience for my decision-making.

My obedience to the Bishop is **THIRD**, and in that order.

In the beginning of this book, the article about St. Francis captured where I am at with the 'Roman' Catholic Church. Like St. Francis, I have chosen to be obedient to the Church and the Hierarchy, but follow Jesus and the Holy Spirit **FIRST**, by simply expressing my disagreement with some of their teachings and practices while still obeying.

As you can imagine, those who lead by use of fear and reprisals to protect their power, have done so to me personally, even though after disagreeing with them, I said I would obey. That mentality **is** the corruption that has infected many in the Hierarchy. In other words, **we have to not only obey them, but agree with them**. This is how evil and power have corrupted them.

**Fear and guilt** have been used for centuries to control the Holy Spirit and believers. I have experienced this as I said before, in the clergy, who are afraid to speak out lest they are declared disobedient and subsequently disciplined.

What do I suggest to those threatened and persecuted this way? Take the position that Jesus took when confronted with this kind of fear.

- *"Jesus of Nazareth, don't you know that **I have the POWER** to set you free, or have you crucified?"* (Jn. 19:10)

When you focus on your **FIRST** commitment, that is to Jesus, who is right there with you, and is your savior and no one else, then he will set you free by using his words to those who have been corrupted by power.

- *"You have no power over me"* (Jn. 19:10)

If you are subjected to reprimand, demeaned, or punished in any way, consider yourself in good company, Jesus, Martin Luther King Jr., Gandhi, Rosa Parks, Nelson Mandela, etc.

- *"Blessed are you when they persecute you and speak all kinds of evil against you for my name. Rejoice, for your reward in heaven will be great."* (Mt. 5:11)

**PS. This does not apply** to all the wonderfully gifted Bishops who love their priests, listen to them, and love their people. Why, because they have been given those gifts, not automatically by their appointment or position, but **by the Holy Spirit**!

## GOD IS DISCIPLINING HIS CHILDREN AND HIS CHURCH, ESPECIALLY THOSE IN AUTHORITY, SEDUCED BY POWER

*"[4] In your struggle against sin, you have not yet resisted to the point of shedding your blood. [5] And have you completely forgotten this word of encouragement that addresses you as a father addresses his son? It says,*

*"My son, do not make light of the Lord's discipline, and do not lose heart when he rebukes you, [6] because the Lord disciplines the one he loves, and he chastens everyone he accepts as his son."*

*[8] If you are not disciplined—and everyone undergoes discipline—then you are not legitimate, not true sons and daughters at all. [9] Moreover, we have all had human fathers who disciplined us and we respected them for it.*

*How much more should we submit to the Father of spirits and live! [10] They disciplined us for a little while as they thought best; but God disciplines us for our good, in order that we may share in his holiness. [11] No discipline seems pleasant at the time, but painful. Later on, however, it produces a harvest of righteousness and peace for those who have been trained by it." (Colossians 1:8).*

Example:
In his letter to the German Hierarchy, quoted earlier, the Pope offered the German Catholic church spiritual counsel and advice as a basis for their work of reform and major changes in their Roman Catholic faith, and encouraged its members—clergy, religious and laity alike—to walk together with Rome and the Universal Church, not alone. Above all, he

emphasized and reminds them of the **central role of the Holy Spirit** in the synod process.

**POINT:** **The Holy Father, Pope Francis, confirms the necessity of experiencing and discerning the Holy Spirit as where the Truth and direction will come from.**

My only question to Pope Francis, and I must confess my frustration with him, is "**Why** doesn't **he** call the 'People of God' who have been Baptized with the Holy Spirit and given the gifts of discernment to meet in Rome or wherever?" What is he waiting for? Like St. Paul said to Timothy, "They have made a pretense of religion, but **deny its Power**."

Why don't they meet, ask, seek, and knock on the door for the Holy Spirit to reveal to them what to do with the evil that has penetrated the church for centuries, to make and create all things new?

What is the hierarchy from top to bottom waiting for, or is it a question of their inability to **let go** of their Power and Trust the Holy Spirit? I wonder! What do you think?

# CHAPTER 12

# PERSONAL SUMMARY

As a Franciscan and ordained priest for 46 years, I love my Catholic faith and tradition. To be honest it has saved my life. The faith and guidance that I got from the priests in my parish as a child and teenager inspired my vocation.

As I look back, they were good men and mentors. When I think back at my experience of the priests and faculty at Wadhams Hall Seminary in Ogdensburg, NY, the education and spiritual guidance was and has been priceless. I've told them over the years that they really saved me. Without the education and spiritual guidance I received there, I probably would have ended up as a tattoo artist in a storefront or blowing up helium balloons in a Dollar Store.

I love all the Catholic traditions that my mother drilled into my older brother, sister, and me, the rosary, lighting candles, novenas, stations of the cross, being an altar server, and even going to confession once a month at the Irish church because my mother told us that they wouldn't know or recognize us there. (Ha Ha), but true.

I loved being part of a church family who knew one another and loved Jesus. I learned how to celebrate each other's presence, have fun at the same time helping with the social events, festivals, and suppers. I learned how to serve the poor, give at thanksgiving and Christmas, and help deliver food for the older people in the parish who were shut-ins. I love the Catholic Church and my Catholicism, and why I am writing this book.

The systemic evil that the Roman empire ushered into the faith whether they knew and intended it or not, has been the source of all the corruption, horrific suffering, killing, sexual immorality and abuse for centuries.

By placing the Holy Spirit and the Sacraments under the umbrella of the Institutional all male hierarchy, they politicized the structure of Christianity, appointing all males to positions of authority as the political and spiritual offices of Priest and Bishop, with all the gifts and dissemination of the Holy Spirit residing solely in them. This reduced a Holy Spirit led people to being just another 'Religion' among many, with a politically established hierarchy in charge.

Satan and evil managed to back into Christianity through the 'original sin' and temptation of **Power**. The only answer to all the evils that have entered people in the Church, especially the Clergy and Hierarchy, is to do as Jesus did with the Pharisees,

- **Call it out**
- **Bind it**
- **Cast it out**, then ask and beg the Holy Spirit for forgiveness and for **a New Pentecost**.


It's not a program, a refresher course for the office of priesthood, or the hierarchy calling another council of the Pope and Bishops to discuss celibacy that is the answer or way forward. That would only be the **all-male political system** trying to save itself, which is exactly what needs to be called out and cast out, to make room for the Holy Spirit to make **'All' things New.**

**Jesus knew that you can't change Evil. It needs to be 'Cast Out'.**

So, like I said when I first started, I'm not a radical, a revolutionary, a heretic, or angry priest, though I confess to a great deal of anger over the years because I saw and felt the damage being done to good faithful brothers and sisters in the name of the church by clergy and Bishops. I myself have been banned by priests and a few bishops because I simply disagreed with them, yet obeyed their decisions.

If the 'Roman' Catholic Church continues to go in this same direction, I am convinced that it will become, if it hasn't already, a Cult, with the Priest and Pastors as the Cult leaders, the only ones who speak for God and have the sole power to disseminate the Holy Spirit and Sacraments.

People will continue to leave, and there will be more and more churches closing, with only those remaining who have no desire to speak out, or are simply content with the Cult mentality and the black and white rules that make them feel safe and secure.

For that 'Roman' Catholic Church, I will continue to pray for the good people and priests that are stuck in it, frustrated and disillusioned.

**I myself have decided to have no part of it**, but have offered in this book the words of Jesus, the power of the Holy Spirit, and the early Christians, as our greatest hope to reform and make all things **New**.

If this does not happen in the near future then I am praying that the Holy Spirit will guide Catholics into the spirituality of the promised 'Remnant' for the end of the age. That is why I have put forth a vision of what that Catholic Church might look like and the Holy Spirit's many gifts to lead and guide it.
Why, so that the world will know that the Father sent Jesus, by the way we Catholics love one another.

### Hallelujah, Come Lord Jesus!

# CREDITS

- Bible, *NIV*

- <u>St. Francis, Reformer, Not A Revolutionary</u>, *Fr. Don Miller, ofm, Jul 19, 2019*

- <u>Face of Jesus</u>, *Mary Jo Woycisjes, Artist, 1976*

- <u>A Brief History of Celibacy in the Catholic Church</u>, *Oxford Dictionary of Popes; H.C. Lea History of Sacerdotal Celibacy in the Christian Church 1957; E. Schillebeeckx The Church with a Human Face 1985; J. McSorley Outline History of the Church by Centuries 1957; F.A.Foy (Ed.) 1990 Catholic Almanac 1989; D.L. Carmody The Double Cross - Ordination, Abortion and Catholic Feminism 1986; P.K. Jewtt The Ordination of Women 1980; A.F. Ide God's Girls - Ordination of Women in the Early Christian & Gnostic Churches 1986*

- <u>*In Came Latin, Incense and Burned Books, Out Went Half The Parishioners Post-Vatican II, North Carolina Catholics Seek A Spiritual Home*</u>, *Jan 27, 2021 by Peter Feuerherd, National Catholic Reporter.*

- Parable 'No Fire', *Unknown source*

- What makes a cult? *Holly Meyer, hmeyer@tennessean.com*

- Vatican News, *Letter to German Bishops*, published 6/9/20

- Cover Picture Mitre, *Expedia.com, Bishops Mitre, Google Images*

- *Pope Francis stripped Vatican Secretariat of financial assets and real estate holdings and assets*, by Nicole Winfield, Associated Press, December 28, 2020

- "Pope Francis' Address to Pontifical Representatives and Apostolic Nuncios". ZENIT. Retrieved 9 June 2017.

- *"Pope: Warns that Poorly Trained Priests Can Become 'Little Monsters'". America Magazine. 4 January 2014. Retrieved 9 June 2017.*

- Photos of St. Francis and Clare, *Franciscan Mystery Players.org, Kennedy Book of the Catholic Directory*

- Francis warns Vatican officials their conflicts polarize Catholic Church, *NCR, December 21, 2020* **Joshua J. McElwee**

- *Holy Spirit clip art, clip-art library.com (Free download)*

**Fr. Francis C. Pompei ofm**
*Author*

**Jesus**
*Co-author*

**Holy Spirit**
*Teacher of all things*

*"Lord, make us instruments of Peace."*

*St. Francis*

www.ingramcontent.com/pod-product-compliance
Lightning Source LLC
Chambersburg PA
CBHW071401290426
44108CB00014B/1641